BUSINESS ECONOMICS IN A RAPIDLY-CHANGING WORLD SERIES

# BACKDATING OF STOCK OPTIONS

# Business Economics in a Rapidly-Changing World Series

**Joint Ventures, Mergers and Acquisitions, and Capital Flow**
*James B. Tobin and Lawrence R. Parker (Editors)*
2009. ISBN: 978-1-60692-795-3

**The Role of Risk and Information in Consumption and Savings**
*Antonella Tutino*
2009. ISBN: 978-1-60741-263-2

**Strategic Economics of Network Industries**
*Hans Gottinger*
2009. ISBN: 978-1-60741-345-5

**Backdating of Stock Options**
*Bernard T. Weinstein (Editor)*
2009. ISBN: 978-1-60741-984-6

**Mark to Market Accounting Standards: A Study by the SEC**
*Brian N. Brinker (Editor)*
2009. ISBN: 978-1-60741-994-5

**Mark to Market and Fair Value Accounting: An Examination**
*James W. Curtis (Editor)*
2009. ISBN: 978-1-60741-996-9

**International Accounting in the 21st Century**
*Aleksei Solovyov and Ilia Kuznetsov (Editor)*
2009. ISBN: 978-1-60876-018-3

**The Role of Corporate Venture Capital in Innovation**
*Joseph F. Tollington (Editors)*
2010. ISBN: 978-1-60876-936-0

**The Role of Corporate Venture Capital in Innovation**
*Joseph F. Tollington (Editors)*
2010. ISBN: 978-1-61668-427-3 (Online Book)

**Multiple Criteria Decision Aiding**
*Constantin Zopounidis, Michael Doumpos, Nikolaos F. Matsatsinis and Evangelos Grigoroudis (Editors)*
2010. ISBN: 978-1-61668-231-6

**Multiple Criteria Decision Aiding**
*Constantin Zopounidis, Michael Doumpos, Nikolaos F. Matsatsinis and Evangelos Grigoroudis (Editors)*
2010. ISBN: 978-1-61668-606-2 (Online Book)

BUSINESS ECONOMICS IN A RAPIDLY-CHANGING WORLD SERIES

# BACKDATING OF STOCK OPTIONS

BERNARD T. WEINSTEIN
EDITOR

**Nova Science Publishers, Inc.**
*New York*

For permission to use material from this book please contact us:
Telephone 631-231-7269; Fax 631-231-8175
Web Site: http://www.novapublishers.com



**LIBRARY OF CONGRESS CATALOGING-IN-PUBLICATION DATA**

*Backdating of stock options / editor, Bernard T. Weinstein.*
*p. cm.*
*Includes index.*
*ISBN 978-1-60741-984-6 (softcover)*
*1. Securities fraud--United States. 2. Stock options--United States. I. Weinstein, Bernard T.*
*HV6763.B33 2009*
*364.16'8--dc22*
*2009038411*

*Published by Nova Science Publishers, Inc. † New York*

# CONTENTS

# PREFACE

This book highlights the issue of backdating of stock options and its ramifications. Employee stock options are contracts giving employees the right to buy the company's common stock at a specified exercise price, at a specified time or during a specified period, and after a specified vesting period. The value of the option when granted lies in the prospect that the market price of the company's stock will increase by the time the option is exercised (used to purchase stock). At the grant date for the options, rather than selecting an exercise price based on the lower market price; that is, they backdated stock options to an earlier grant date. If this backdating occurred without public disclosure, the recipient of the stock options received increased compensation in violation of Securities and Exchange Commission (SEC) regulations, generally accepted accounting rules, and tax laws. Some backdating is said to involve "sloppiness," not fraud. The backdating of stock options has imposed costs on shareholders, employees, bondholders and taxpayers. This book consists of public documents which have been located, gathered, combined, reformatted, and enhanced with a subject index, selectively edited and bound to provide easy access.

Chapter 1 - Employee stock options are contracts giving employees the right to buy the company's common stock at a specified exercise price, at a specified time or during a specified period, and after a specified vesting period. The value of the option when granted lies in the prospect that the market price of the company's stock will increase by the time the option is exercised (used to purchase stock). At the grant date for the options, rather than selecting an exercise price based on the current market price for the stock, officials at some companies have selected a prior date with a lower market price; that is, they *backdated* stock options to an earlier grant date. If this backdating occurred *without public disclosure*, the recipient of the stock options received increased compensation in violation of Securities and Exchange Commission (SEC) regulations, generally accepted accounting rules, and tax laws. Some backdating is said to involve "sloppiness," not fraud. The backdating of stock options has imposed costs on shareholders, employees, bondholders, and taxpayers.

Chapter 2 is a transcript of a speech given by a member of the U. S. Securities and Exchange Commission staff.

Chapters 3 through 7 feature testimony before the U. S. Senate.

In: Backdating of Stock Options
Editor: Bernard T. Weinstein
ISBN: 978-1-60741-984-6


*Chapter 1*

# STOCK OPTIONS: THE BACKDATING ISSUES*

***James M. Bickley[1] and Gary Shorter[2]***
[1]Public Finance
[2]Financial Economics

## SUMMARY

Employee stock options are contracts giving employees the right to buy the company's common stock at a specified exercise price, at a specified time or during a specified period, and after a specified vesting period. The value of the option when granted lies in the prospect that the market price of the company's stock will increase by the time the option is exercised (used to purchase stock). At the grant date for the options, rather than selecting an exercise price based on the current market price for the stock, officials at some companies have selected a prior date with a lower market price; that is, they *backdated* stock options to an earlier grant date. If this backdating occurred *without public disclosure*, the recipient of the stock options received increased compensation in violation of Securities and Exchange Commission (SEC) regulations, generally accepted accounting rules, and tax laws. Some backdating is said to involve "sloppiness," not fraud. The backdating of stock

* This is an edited, reformatted and augmented version of a CRS Report for Congress publication dated February 2009.

options has imposed costs on shareholders, employees, bondholders, and taxpayers.

A corporate official who has profited from undisclosed backdating of stock options may not be responsible or even knowledgeable of the backdating. "Nonqualified" stock options, which have no special tax criteria to meet, are the focus of the backdating controversy primarily because they can be granted in unlimited amounts.

The magnitude of stock option grants grew dramatically in the 1990s, subsequent to passage of the Omnibus Budget Reconciliation Act of 1993, a stock market boom, and revised accounting rules. Recent corporate disclosure changes have reduced the opportunities and rewards for backdating stock options. Empirical studies about backdating have been done by academics and investigative journalists.

Four regulatory actions may have reduced the backdating of stock options, but problems persist. On December 16, 2004, the Financial Accounting Standards Board issued new rules requiring companies to subtract the expense of options from their earnings. After August 29, 2002, the Sarbanes-Oxley Act required that companies notify the SEC within two business days after granting stock options. In 2003, the SEC required increased disclosure of stock option plans. The SEC issued enhanced option grant disclosure rules effective December 15, 2006. Policy options to further reduce backdating and other timing manipulation include changes in SEC regulations and a change in the tax law.

The SEC, various state prosecutorial, and Department of Justice (DOJ) probes into backdating abuses are ongoing. In addition, many firms have mounted their own internal probes into possible abuses. By November 2007, the SEC's investigation caseload declined from a peak of 160 to about 80 (as reported in *Financial Week*). Between 2007 and 2008, SEC enforcement actions show that new backdating charges against officials of corporations declined from 11 to 8 and outof-court settlements rose from 7 to 10. As of January 30, 2009, the only chief executive officer (CEO) to be convicted of charges related to backdating and sentenced to prison was Greg Reyes, former Brocade CEO. The SEC has been emphasizing out-of-court settlements rather than prosecutions. New backdating charges against corporate officials will likely continue to decline in 2009.

This chapter will be updated as issues develop or new legislation is introduced.

# INTRODUCTION

Employee stock options are contracts giving employees (including officers), and sometimes directors and other service providers, the right to buy the company's common stock at a specified *exercise price or strike price* at a specified time or during a specified period after a specified vesting period. Options have most often been issued "at-the-money" (i.e., with an exercise price equal to the market price of the underlying stock at the date of grant) but may also be issued either "in-the-money" (i.e., with an exercise price below the market price of the underlying stock at the date of grant) or "out-of-the-money" (i.e., with an exercise price above the market price of the underlying stock at the date of grant). The intrinsic value of the option is the market value of the stock less the exercise price, which is only relevant if the stock option is issued *in the money*. The time value of the option when granted lies in the prospect that the market price of the company's stock will increase by the time the option is exercised (used to purchase stock); that is, its potential appreciation value. Setting a lower exercise price increases the value of the option.

At the grant date for the options, rather than selecting an exercise or strike price based on the current market price for the stock, officials at some companies have selected a prior date with a lower market price; that is, they *backdated* stock options to an earlier date. Thus, officials backdated the grant date of the option (e.g., on January 10 the company's officials decided to grant stock options as of January 5), which resulted in stock options being granted *in the money*.

If backdating occurred *without disclosure*, then the recipient of the stock options receives an increase in compensation at the expense of other shareholders when he exercises his options to purchase stock. Undisclosed backdating of stock options violates regulations of the Securities and Exchange Commission (SEC), accounting rules, and tax laws.

Failure to disclose backdating and recognize adverse tax and accounting consequences may result in (1) material errors in financial statements, fraud and other violations of securities law, including falsifying books and records; and misrepresenting financial filings to auditors—central concerns of the SEC (with respect to violations of civil law) and the Department of Justice (with respect to violations of criminal law); and (2) the loss of tax deductions and imposition of penalties and interest for failure to withhold and accurately report income and employment taxes—central concerns of the Internal Revenue Service (IRS).[1]

Backdating the grant date could be undertaken for innocent reasons (e.g., to provide equity for recently-hired employees when stock prices are volatile) that were undertaken in ignorance of the negative accounting and tax complications.[2] Backdating is not necessarily illegal. The SEC has resource constraints and thus is limited in the number of backdating cases that it can pursue.

According to Stephen J. Crimmins, formerly of SEC's Enforcement Division and co-manager of its Trial Unit, as the SEC pursues the stock option cases,

> it will be particularly interesting to see how the government handles situations where individuals did not knowingly violate the law or deceptively cover up their activities, where individuals lacked an understanding of the accounting and tax rules involved in option grants, where they relied on in-house or outside professionals to alert them to potential compliance issues, and where problems stemmed from imprecision or outright sloppiness in tending to the formalities that drive the setting of grant dates.[3]

By November 2007, the SEC's backdating investigation caseload declined from a peak of 160 firms to about 80.[4] About 200 companies were under federal investigation and/or have restated earnings.[5] And by November 2007, the SEC has brought civil enforcement actions against seven companies and 26 former executives associated with 15 firms and the Department of Justice (DOJ) has reportedly brought at least 10 criminal filings against defendants for backdating.[6] As of January 30, 2009, the only chief executive officer (CEO) to be convicted of charges related to backdating and sentenced to prison was Greg Reyes, former Brocade CEO.[7]

As of January 30, 2009, by far the largest backdating abuse settlement involved a December 2007 agreement involving William McGuire, former chairman and CEO of UnitedHealth Group Inc., the nation's largest health managed care firm. His repayment of $468 million represents the first SEC-sanctioned use of Section 304 (the "clawback" provision) of the Sarbanes-Oxley Act of 2002 against an individual. The provision is aimed at depriving executives of stock profits and bonuses earned while misleading investors. Mr. McGuire also agreed to pay a $7 million fine in an agreement yesterday with the U.S. Securities and Exchange Commission related to the alleged backdating.[8] As part of the settlement, Mr. McGuire neither admitted nor denied wrongdoing.[9]

Some executives at other firms are under SEC, state prosecutorial, and Justice Department scrutiny. It is uncertain how many of these probes will ultimately result in criminal or civil charges, or SEC penalties. The SEC has been emphasizing out-of-court settlements rather than prosecutions. Between 2007 and 2008, SEC enforcement actions show that new backdating charges against officials of corporations declined from 11 to 8 and out-of-court settlements rose from 7 to 10.[10] New backdating charges against corporate officials will likely continue to decline in 2009.

While undisclosed backdating of stock options is the focus of this chapter and the most important type of timing manipulation, it should be noted that there are other forms of timing manipulation, which are discussed in **Appendix A**. In some cases when more than one form of timing manipulation occurs, it may be difficult to empirically separate the relative magnitude of the cost to the shareholders of these different forms of manipulation, including backdating.

In order to fully understand the backdating issue, this chapter covers the following topics: illustration of undisclosed backdating, types of stock options, growth of stock options in the 1990s, the extent of timing manipulation of options, the potential costs of backdating, key legislative and regulatory developments, gatekeepers, and potential policy options.

## ILLUSTRATION OF UNDISCLOSED BACKDATING

A hypothetical case of undisclosed backdating is shown in the following example, which demonstrates violations of laws and regulations. It should be emphasized that backdating can take a variety of forms, and in some cases an employee may not be aware that his stock options have been backdated.

Assume that ABC, Inc. is a publicly held corporation whose stock is selling for $50 a share on December 31, 1998. As a part of his compensation plan, ABC, Inc.'s chief executive officer (CEO) is granted options on that date to buy 10,000 shares of stock for $50 a share (at the money). But, without disclosure, the CEO knowingly selects a prior grant date of August 15, 1998, when the stock price was at its low for the year ($30).[11] In other words, the grant date has been *backdated*, resulting in a reduced exercise price of $30. Because of backdating, in 1998, the CEO received an undisclosed gain on paper of $20 ($50—$30) per share for a total of $200,000 ($20 X 10,000). This gain was not indicated in the financial statements of the corporation in 1998. Shareholders were unaware of the backdating, which occurred at their expense. This undisclosed gain is not consistent with the options agreement that the company filed with the SEC.

Assume that the vesting period is two years and any time over the next eight years he may exercise his options. Thus, from the time the stock options are granted until the final date of exercise is 10 years. On December 31, 2000, his options become vested; that is, he receives an unrestricted right to buy 10,000 shares of stock for $30 a share. Assume that on December 31, 2000, the stock price is $75. He decides to exercise his options. (He could have delayed exercising his options at any time until December 31, 2008). He pays ABC $300,000 ($30 X 10,000). He has an immediate gain of $450,000 ($45 X 10,000 shares) on paper. Assuming that these are nonqualified stock options,[12] in the year that the options are exercised (2000), the CEO owes taxes on the gain in value and ABC, Inc. deducts only $300,000 as the cost of these options. Thus the actual cost of the options to the company is understated. The CEO has the choice of selling some (or all) of his shares or delaying their sale with the hope that the price of the stock will rise further.

## TYPES OF STOCK OPTIONS

The Internal Revenue Code (IRC) recognizes two fundamental types of options. One is "nonqualified" options, which have no special tax criteria to meet, but are taxed to the employee as wage income when their value can be unambiguously established (which IRS says is when they are no longer at risk of forfeiture and can be freely transferred).[13] They are deductible by the employer when the employee includes them in income (IRC Section 83). The other is called "statutory" or "qualified" options, which are accorded favorable tax treatment if they meet the IRC's strict qualifications (IRC Section 421-424). Qualified stock options are excluded from employment (payroll) taxes.

### Nonqualified Stock Options

Nonqualified options may be granted in unlimited amounts; these are the options making the news as creating large fortunes for some officers and highly paid employees and are the focus of the backdating controversy. In addition to employees, these options may also be awarded to anyone "providing services" to the company, including members of the board of directors and even independent contractors. They are taxed when exercised and all restrictions on selling the stock have expired, based on the difference between the price paid for the stock and its market value at exercise. The company is allowed a deduction for the same amount in the year the employee includes it in income; that is, in the same year it is taxable to the recipient. They are subject to employment taxes also. Although taxes are postponed on nonqualified options until they are exercised, the deduction allowed the company is also postponed, so there is generally little if any tax advantage to these options. Since most of these options go to highly compensated individuals, whose marginal tax rates are approximately equal to the company's, the government probably suffers little if any revenue loss. The justification for the postponement of taxes on the recipient and the deduction to the corporation is the uncertainty of their actual value; the tax rules follow the practical path of postponing tax until their value is realized, as is the case with capital gains.

## Qualified Stock Options

Qualified (or "statutory") options include "incentive stock options," which are limited to $100,000 a year for any one employee, and "employee stock purchase plans," which are limited to $25,000 a year for any qualified employee. Employee stock purchase plans must be offered to all full-time employees with at least two years of service; incentive stock options may be confined to officers and highly paid employees. Qualified options are not taxed to the employee when granted or exercised (under the regular tax); tax is imposed only when the stock is sold. If the stock is held one year from purchase and two years from the granting of the option, the gain is taxed as long-term capital gain. The employer is not allowed a deduction for these options. However, if the stock is not held the required time, the employee is taxed at ordinary income tax rates and the employer is allowed a deduction. The value of incentive stock options is included in minimum taxable income in the year of exercise.[14]

# Growth of Stock Options in the 1990s

The magnitude of stock option grants grew dramatically in the 1990s because of the passage of the Omnibus Budget Reconciliation Act of 1993, the stock market boom, and changes in accounting rules.

## The Omnibus Budget Reconciliation Act of 1993

The Tax Reform Act of 1986 broadened the individual income tax base and lowered marginal tax rates. It can be argued that the Omnibus Budget Reconciliation Act of 1993 (P.L. 103-66) made two changes in the tax law that contributed to a substantial increase in the granting of stock options to corporate executives: higher marginal income tax rates and a deductibility cap of $1 million on applicable compensation.

### *Higher Marginal Individual Income Tax Rates*

The Omnibus Budget Reconciliation Act of 1993 raised marginal individual income tax rates, which had a current maximum rate of 28%. The new maximum marginal tax rate was 39.6%. The stated reasons for raising marginal income tax rates were "to raise revenue to reduce the federal deficit, to improve tax equity, and to make the individual income tax system more progressive."[15] These higher marginal income tax rates gave an incentive to individuals to receive types of remuneration that would be taxed at a lower rate. Some returns on stock options are subject to the long-term capital gains rate. In addition, some individuals can defer redeeming stock options until their marginal tax rate declines. The importance of higher marginal tax rates was lessened, however, by the reductions in marginal rates during the Bush Administration—the highest marginal tax rate for 2008 is 35%.[16]

### *"Excessive Remuneration"— Section 162(m)*

The Omnibus Budget Reconciliation Act of 1993 established code section 162(m), titled "Certain Excessive Employee Remuneration," which applied to the CEO and the four highest compensated officers (other than the CEO) of a publicly held corporation. For each of these "covered employees," the publicly held corporation could only deduct, as an expense, the first $1 million of applicable remuneration. The reason for this change was that "the committee believes that excessive compensation will be reduced if the deduction for compensation ... paid to the top executives of publicly held corporations is limited to $1 million per year."[17] Exceptions to this $1 million in applicable remuneration include (1) "remuneration payable on commission basis" and (2) "other performance-based compensation." In order to qualify for this second exception, four conditions must be met:

- It is paid solely on account of the attainment of one or more performance goals.
- The performance goals are determined by a compensation committee of the board of directors of the taxpayer, which is comprised solely of two or more outside directors.
- The material terms under which the remuneration is to be paid, including the performance goals, are disclosed to shareholders and approved by a majority of the vote in a separate shareholder vote before the payment of such remuneration.
- Before any payment of such remuneration, the compensation committee certifies that the performance goals and any other material terms were in fact satisfied.[18]

Undisclosed backdating of stock option grants in the money is not "disclosed to shareholders and approved by a majority of the vote in a separate shareholder vote before the payment of such remuneration"; hence, the third condition is not met.

Economic theory suggests that the $1 million cap on deductible compensation would increase the relative importance of performance-related compensation including stock options.[19] In retrospect, the provision appears to have made stock options relatively less expensive than base salaries, bonuses, or stock grants, which were subject to the cap.

With the backdating scandals as a catalyst, a number of policymakers sought to examine some of the policy implications of the law. Charles Grassley, former Chairman of the Senate Finance Committee, has said

> companies have found it easy to get around the law. It has more holes than Swiss cheese. And it seems to have encouraged the options industry. These sophisticated folks are working with Swiss watch-like devices to game this Swiss cheese-like rule. I want to know what went wrong and consider whether it makes sense to make changes.[20]

SEC Chairman Christopher Cox testified that

> I well remember that the stated purpose [of the tax law] was to control the rate of growth in CEO pay. With complete hindsight, we can now all agree that this purpose was not achieved. Indeed, this tax law change deserves pride of place in the museum of unintended consequences.[21]

### The Stock Market Boom of the 1990s

The substantial stock market advances of the 1990s provided a significant boost to the attraction of option awards. It could also be argued that because shareholders also benefitted from the market's gains, their inclination to criticize the growing size of executive option grants may have been reduced.[22]

### Cost Accounting Rules for Certain Stock Options

Going into the 1990s, companies had the choice of recognizing the estimated value of stock options grants commonly awarded to executives and rank and file workers as costs in their income statements or simply disclosing option grants in the footnotes to the financial statements, where they had no impact on reported earnings. Most opted to do so via the footnote disclosure. In 1991, the Financial Accounting Standards Board (FASB), the private sector entity that writes accounting rules, proposed that an estimated value of such stock options be a mandatory cost item in a firm's financial statements. But after vigorous corporate opposition, particularly from high tech industry firms, FASB opted not to adopt the proposal until 2004. Many have since argued that had the proposal been adopted earlier, firms might have been less generous in their executive option grant awards.[23]

## THE EXTENT OF TIMING MANIPULATION OF OPTIONS

The literature on timing manipulation of stock option grants is extensive. Major empirical studies of timing manipulation other than backdating are summarized in **Appendix D**. These studies find strong statistical support for the hypothesis that some CEOs have arranged for their award of stock options to occur shortly before a positive public announcement by their company (springloading). Other studies have statistically verified the hypothesis that some executives controlled the flow of both positive and negative news around dates of scheduled grants of options. Another study found statistical support for the hypothesis that executives timed the repricing of stock options based on the release of corporate news.

This chapter focuses on the backdating of the grant date for stock options. The relevant literature, which is summarized in **Appendix C**, is divided between academic studies and empirical analyses in *The Wall Street Journal*. The first academic study was undertaken in 2004 by Professor Erik Lie, who found strong econometric evidence of extensive backdating. His subsequent work with Professor Randall A. Heron found that between January 1, 1996, and December 1, 2005, 29% of 7,774 companies engaged in timing manipulation (primarily backdating) in granting stock options to top executives. Other studies examined the role of outside directors and the effect of the options backdating scandal on stock-price performance of companies.

## THE POTENTIAL COSTS OF BACKDATING

Corporate executives appear to have profited handsomely from undisclosed backdating, although they may ultimately be faced with a number of costs related to such actions.[24] However, there is clear evidence of backdating's direct or indirect costs to specific entities, including shareholders, employees, bondholders, and taxpayers. This section describes such costs.

### Costs to Shareholders

In general terms, the undisclosed backdating of stock options secretly transfers wealth from a company's shareholders to its option recipients, understating a company's expenses, and overstating net profits. When options are exercised, companies always receive less than what the shares are worth on the open market. Backdating increases this cost.

#### *Costs from Earnings Hits*

Firms where backdating is detected may have to adjust to the accounting shortfall by downward restatements of previous earnings disclosures. Public announcement that a restatement may be forthcoming usually has a strong negative effect on share prices. As mentioned in the introduction, an empirical study concluded that the options backdating scandal had reduced the value of the stock of 110 corporations by at least $100 billion.[25]

### *Costs of Reduced Executive Performance*

By artificially lowering an option's exercise price, backdating can reduce some of a stock option's performance incentive effects on executives. Backdating the grant date of the options reduces the exercise price below the market price on the day of the award and gives an executive an immediate windfall. This means that over a certain share price range, there is no linkage between an executive's potential gain from an option award and the performance of the underlying stock.

Officials of firms involved in backdating probes may find that a significant amount of their time is diverted to probe-related matters, taking them away from more conventional corporate concerns. In more extreme circumstances, some corporate executives have been fired or forced to step down, introducing the prospect of corporate inefficiencies due to leadership discontinuities.

### *Costs from Delistings*

Shareholders risk additional losses if the stock is delisted. Exchange bylaws call for the delisting of companies that fail to release required quarterly or annual financial disclosures on time. But due to internal option probes, it has been reported that nearly 50 firms with market capitalizations of $75 million or more had postponed their quarterly filings for the second quarter of 2006. By October of that year, it was reported that 54 firms had been told that they faced potential delistings for such delays. Several companies have had their stock delisted by Nasdaq for failing to publish audited financial reports on time due to problems with backdating of options. Delisting is usually followed by a sharp drop in associated share price, and delisted firms tend to face increased borrowing costs. If they migrate to another trading venue, it is generally a more marginal entity like the OTC Bulletin Board or the Pink Sheets, markets generally associated with low and volatile stock prices, and high trading costs.[26]

### *Costs from the Actions of Bondholders*

Shareholders may experience financial losses due to bondholders demanding payments for breached indentures. Corporate bonds normally contain an indenture, a detailed contract between the issuer and the debt holders that requires the firm to file quarterly and annual reports with those holders at or around the same time it files with the SEC. This means that late filers, including many of the firms undergoing backdating probes, may be in technical default of their indentures. Historically, however, the convention has generally been that in such cases debt holders give the issuers adequate time to work things out. But there are reports that some bondholders, including hedge funds, have targeted a number of firms with delayed filings due to backdating concerns, and are either demanding immediate payment of the value of the debt or requiring the borrowers to pay substantial fees. For example, in the summer of 2006, Amkor Technology came close to missing the deadline for paying bondholders who had demanded repayment of more than $1.5 billion in debt. And during the same summer, the Sanmina-SCI Corporation asked its bondholders for an extension on the terms of its indenture, offering them financial concessions of $12.5 million.

### *Costs of Additional Taxes*

Firms found to have been involved in abusive backdating may also incur additional tax expenses because the pay to their top five executives is not eligible for the same tax deductions that performance-based options are if the options they receive do not depend on a performance measure like an appreciation in the stock price after the option grant. Backdated options confer immediate paper profits and are not treated like performance-based options, making them ineligible for such deductions.

### *Costs of Probes, Fines, and Lawsuits*

Firms that decide to conduct internal backdating probes can incur significant costs. In addition, the ongoing SEC, Department of Justice (DOJ), and IRS probes may result in certain firms facing significant fines.[27] A growing number of firms currently face backdating-based shareholder suits that allege either breach of fiduciary duty or violation of anti-fraud provisions of the U.S. Securities Exchange Act of 1934. The suits consume corporate resources in the form of legal expenses and may result in significant money judgments against the firms. Again, these are expended funds that cannot be reinvested in longer-term, potentially share-price-enhancing corporate growth or distributed as shareholder dividends

## Employees

Some employees may not be aware that their stock options have been backdated. Consequently, they may be liable "for unanticipated tax as well as interest and penalties."[28] Some companies distributed stock options to many levels of employees without disclosing to these employees (or the public) that their options had been backdated.[29] Some of these employees with gains on their incentive stock options (ISO) may have paid only capital gains taxes rather than regular income tax on the rise in value due to backdating. Now, these employees may owe the difference between the higher regular income tax and the capital gains tax, plus interest.[30] Furthermore, these employees may owe additional payroll taxes because backdating cancels an exemption from ISOs from payroll taxes. If an employee's stock options vested after December 2004, then-section 409A of the tax code applies, and tax is due when options vest rather than when they were exercised. Thus, these employees may also be liable for a 20% penalty and interest.[31]

## Bondholders

A number of firms that have grappled with publicly disclosed backdating concerns have seen their debt trade at substantial discounts to par value, which can mean a loss in value for their debtholders. Bond raters may lower the debt ratings of firms that are confronting backdating problems. Lower rated debt raises the cost of corporate financing.

## Taxpayers

If recipients of backdated stock options underpay their taxes, then taxpayers in general lose. In order to raise a given amount of revenue, these other taxpayers must pay higher taxes. Some corporate executives have not reported the backdated basis price, and thus understated the realized gain on the sale of stock and underpaid their income tax. Some corporations involved in backdating have claimed deductions for executive remuneration above the $1 million limit that was not performance related. For qualified options, if some employees are able to illegally obtain additional compensation from backdating in the form of long-term capital gains, then tax revenue is lost because the marginal tax rate on long-term capital gains is below that on regular income. Also, taxpayers must cover the cost of litigation in prosecuting undisclosed backdating cases.

## KEY LEGISLATIVE AND REGULATORY DEVELOPMENTS

Several major legislative and regulatory developments may have reduced the use of options in the aggregate, and thus reduced options-related abuse, but they are not aimed at backdating per se.

### Sarbanes-Oxley Act: Stock Option Disclosure Reforms

Enacted in the wake of widespread accounting scandals at firms like Enron and WorldCom, the Sarbanes-Oxley Act of 2002 (SOX) contained a host of corporate governance and accounting regulatory reforms. Prior to SOX, firm insiders were required to disclose grants of stock options within 45 days of the end of a company's fiscal year. SOX requires that all insider transactions in a company's stock, including option grants, be disclosed within two business days. The requirement went into effect on August 29, 2002.

In a number of instances, this "fiscal year plus 45-day" reporting window may have given companies time to review their earlier stock price performance, identify the low point, and retroactively designate that date as the stock option grant date. After August 29, 2002, the Sarbanes-Oxley Act required that companies notify the SEC within two business days after granting stock options. This requirement reduced the frequency of backdating and the magnitude of the gains to executives from backdating. But many companies fail to file the required Form 4 within the two-day period.[32]

## SEC's 2003 Requirement of Approval of Compensation Plans

In 2003, the SEC approved changes to the listing standards of the New York Stock Exchange and the Nasdaq Stock Market that require shareholder approval of almost all equity-based compensation plans. Firms must disclose the material terms of their stock option plans, prior to obtaining shareholder approval for them. The required disclosures include the terms on which options will be granted, including whether the plan permits options to be granted with an exercise price that is below market value on the date of the grant.

## American Jobs Creation Act of 2004 (Section 409A)

The American Jobs Creation Act of 2004 (P.L. 108-357) included new statutory requirements under Code Section 409A concerning deferred compensation, that is, the delay of the receipt of compensation and taxes on compensation to a future tax year. This section was included "in response to perceived abuses by executive employees in the recent wave of corporate scandals."[33]

This section applies to amounts deferred in tax years that begin after December 31, 2004 and includes stock appreciation rights if the exercise price is less than the fair market value of the underlying stock on the date the stock appreciation rights are granted.[34] Section 409A generally provides that

> amounts deferred under a nonqualified deferred compensation plan for all taxable years are currently includible in gross income to the extent not subject to substantial risk of forfeiture and not previously included in gross income, unless certain requirements are met.[35]

Thus, stock options, subject to 409 A, were included in income when they vested rather than when they were exercised. Consequently, Code Section 409A reduced the tax advantage of stock options, and presumably reduced the use of stock options.

## FASB Rule for Expensing Stock Options

On December 16, 2004, the Financial Accounting Standards Board issued new rules [FAS 123(R)] requiring companies to subtract the expense of the estimated value of their option grants from their earnings as disclosed in their financial statements.[36] The requirement, which applies to the fiscal years beginning April 21, 2005, meant that firms could no longer choose between formally expensing the estimated value of their options grants or merely disclosing that value in footnotes. For many companies, especially the high tech firms that extensively issued options to their rank and file workers as well as their executives, the rule dramatically reduces their reported net earnings. In the rule's aftermath, grants of executive options are still quite substantial but the rule ( in conjunction with other factors like the end of the 1990s stock market boom) has helped reduce the overall level of option awards.[37]

## SEC's 2006 Executive Compensation Disclosure Rules

While the aforementioned initiatives may have played a role in reducing the incidence of abusive backdating, a July 2006 SEC rule making, which went into effect in 2007, may have a salutary future effect in this area.[38] It consisted of a package of rules designed to enhance the transparency of proxy compensation disclosures for CEOs, chief financial officers (CFOs), the other three highest paid executive officers, and directors, the first such major reform since 1992. Passing no judgment on the practice's legality or illegality, the rules include provisions that require companies to disclose whether they are timing options grants to make them more lucrative to executives and other employees.[39]

The rules require companies to present, in tabular form, the stock price on the grant date, the grant date under accounting rules, the market price on the grant date if it is greater than the exercise price, and the date the compensation committee or full board granted the award if different than the grant date for accounting purposes. In a new section of the proxy, *Compensation Discussion and Analysis*, management must discuss material information such as the reasons a company selects particular grant dates for awards and the methods a company uses to set the terms of awards.

To provide investors with a better handle on firms' use of springloading (issuing options just before the release of good news, a practice which is not illegal per se), the rules also require management to answer questions such as,

- Does the company coordinate the timing of option grants to executives, including new executives, with the release of material nonpublic information?
- How does any such program fit in with granting options to employees more generally?
- What role did the compensation committee and executive officers play in such a plan? and
- Does a company plan to time, or has it timed, its release of material nonpublic information for the purpose of affecting the value of executive compensation?[40]

SEC officials have said that along with the aforementioned two-day option award reporting requirement ushered in by SOX, the new executive disclosure rules should inject more transparency into the option grant award process and should essentially eliminate "easy opportunities to get away with secretive options grants."[41] Agency officials and other observers have also indicated that largely due to the tightened option award window required by SOX, the opportunity for corporate officials to retroactively date option awards appears to have been all but eliminated.[42]

But several recent academic studies suggest that this sanguine view may be overstated and perhaps somewhat premature. The research found that although the incidence of backdating appears to have been greatly reduced, a relatively small but not insignificant level of option grant manipulation still persists, manipulation that likely includes backdating.[43]

Furthermore, critics argue that the new proxy tables do not include all stock options data because of two factors.[44] First , before FAS 123(R) took effect, over 900 companies accelerated the vesting of stock options to collectively erase about $8 billion of future stock option expenses from their books.[45] Second, in December 2006, the SEC changed a rule to allow corporations "to report the amount of stock options that vest per year rather than the total value of the options granted to an executive."[46]

# GATEKEEPERS

A number of entities are commonly viewed as general protectors of investors' interests, a responsibility that arguably becomes more pronounced with the prospect of corporate misconduct such as abusive backdating. This section examines the roles of key "gatekeepers"—corporate boards, their compensation committees, outside auditors, and the SEC.

## Corporate Boards and Compensation Committees

Among other things, corporate boards, particularly their non-managerial members known as outside directors, are responsible for upholding shareholders' interests vis-a-vis potentially self- serving executive behavior. This view is reflected in a number of statutory and regulatory rules, including requirements that only outside directors serve on board audit and compensation committees.

A corporate board generally possesses the ultimate authority for determining and overseeing the compensation of its key executives. A majority of the board may, however, broadly delegate that authority to board committees. Typically, such authority is delegated to the compensation committee which is responsible for (1) recommending compensation programs and pay levels for the CEO and other top executives; (2) approving employment agreements and other contracts with such executives; and (3) administering equity-based and other long-term incentive compensation plans, including option grants.

When a compensation committee recommends option-based compensation for company executives, the firm's board then adopts a stock option plan describing the basic terms of the plan. Option plans typically say that the options will have exercise prices close to the prevailing share price on either the day they are awarded or the preceding day.

In most cases, option plans are then submitted to the company's stockholders for approval as required by the exchange listing requirements discussed above. After approval of the plans, responsibility for overseeing the provision of option grant awards to specific individuals tends generally rests with compensation committees.

Corporate boards are thus integral to the option grant award process. And the centrality of this role—combined with the fact that historically CEOs have had significant influence in the selection of board members—has raised concerns over director complicity and oversight in the backdating scandals.[47]

An examination of articles on various firms embroiled in options backdating reveals a wide spectrum of potential board involvement and non-involvement in improprieties involving backdating. For example, there have been reports of board members: (1) being duped by firm executives who manipulated the option grant dates; (2) giving executives blanket approval in the choice of their own option grant dates; and (3) being very much "out of the loop" with respect to the "nuts and bolts" responsibilities over options issuance (which could raise issues over the effectiveness of the board's oversight).

An exhaustive study of option grant awards to the outside directors of publicly traded firms between 1996 and 2005 found that a substantial number of directors have benefitted from suspiciously timed option grant awards, raising concerns over director involvement in backdating abuse. The study, by a group that included Lucien Bebchuk, director of the Harvard Law School Program on Corporate Governance, examined 29,000 option grants given to 1,400 outside directors and found that 9% (or approximately 800) were granted on the day of the lowest monthly share price. The likelihood of such a large percentage of grants occurring on monthly lows was so statistically improbable that the authors concluded that these "lucky grants" were evidence of deliberate and opportunistic timing.[48]

The authors' conclusion that the timing was generally deliberate in nature appears to have been buttressed by the finding that grant events were more likely to be "lucky" during months in which the difference between the median price and the lowest price was the greatest. The research also found that when the award dates for directors' grants coincided with those for the executives, especially the CEO, the director grants were more likely to be lucky. The study did not address key questions surrounding the backdating abuse such as who was responsible, who knew what, and the mindset of the parties involved.

Still, such findings raise fundamental concerns over the effectiveness of many outside directors as shareholder guardians vis-a-vis potentially self-dealing executives. The research also raises important corollary concerns about the adequacy of corporate governance structures and protocol. For example, the director grant study also finds that firms lacking a majority of outside directors were more likely to award lucky grants to their board members.[49]

In another study, the same authors examined executive option grant awards issued by several thousand firms between 1996 and 2006 and found that lucky CEO grants were more apt to occur when a firm lacked a majority of outside directors. That research also determined that the longer a CEO's tenure, the greater the prospect of option manipulation, probably reflecting that executive influence over board composition and behavior may tend to grow over time.[50] Another study examined the firm characteristics that help influence the extent to which CEO's wield power and influence over their boards and compensation committees, and found evidence suggesting that weaker corporate governance tends to increase the likelihood that executive option grants will be backdated.[51]

As of February 3, 2009, a number of directors have been sued in civil court, and some directors have resigned their positions. But board members outside of CEOs who also served as board chairs have not been implicated in backdates abuses with the exception of Michael Shanahan Jr., a former member of the board of directors and the compensation committee of Engineered Support Systems. In July 2007, Mr. Shanahan was one of three firm officials who were indicted by a federal grand jury in St. Louis on multiple counts of fraud in connection with a stock options backdating scheme.[52]

## Utside Auditors

To comply with U.S. securities laws, and to help ensure their financial accountability and to help identify weaknesses in their internal controls and systems, companies contract with independent accountants known as external auditors or outside accountants to conduct an audit of their financial statements, records, transactions, and operations. The most common kind of audit is a financial statement audit, which judges the reliability of the data in the financial report in light of generally accepted accounting principles.

As such, outside auditors are widely expected to serve a "watchdog" role over the integrity of a firm's internal accounting. Like the massive corporate financial reporting problems at firms like Enron and Worldcom that led to the Sarbanes-Oxley Act and major accounting regulatory reform, some of the abusive backdating appears to involve faulty financial disclosure.

Most backdaters failed to make accurate disclosures, putting them in a position of potential noncompliance with GAAP.[53] When such problems emerge, questions are invariably raised about the role played by the outside auditors.[54]

At this juncture, there is a wide range of speculation on the roles that outside auditors may have played in the corporate backdating misconduct. For example, one notion is that outside auditors should not have been expected to question the veracity of firm documents showing particular option grant dates. But a more critical perspective is that the auditors may have regarded options-based accounting reporting as a low-risk concern, approaching these concerns in a cursory and superficial way, at best, and taking companies' reporting at face value and expending little effort to confirm the documents' veracity, at worst.[55]

Research conducted by Eric Lie and Randall Heron found that among large and small accounting firms, PricewaterhouseCoopers and KPMG were associated with a lower percentage of stock option manipulation.[56] It also found little evidence that accounting firms actually promoted backdating to their audit clients, as some have alleged. The study also concluded that smaller auditors in contrast to larger ones were associated with a larger proportion of option grant award disclosures that were tardily filed, as well as unscheduled option grant awards,[57] which are more apt to lead to backdating.

One of the broad objectives of the Sarbanes-Oxley Act of 2002 was to help ensure that corporate audits are performed in an independent manner devoid of self-serving corporate bias. To date, the preponderance of the backdating being probed appears to have taken place before the enactment of the act. While many feel that the act's expedited option grant award reporting provision has virtually eliminated current backdating abuse, others are less convinced. And to the extent that this view proves credible, questions could be raised anew about the extent to which the act has led to greater auditing accountability in areas such as this.

## Securities and Exchange Commission

As indicated earlier, along with the IRS and the DOJ, the SEC is currently involved in a number of backdating investigations. SEC officials have said that if Congress saw fit to provide it with additional resources for its work in this area, the funds would be put to good use.[58] The SEC faces the perennial challenge of marshaling adequate resources to deal with capital markets that continue to grow in both complexity and scope. Agency officials have said that they have sufficient resources to adequately pursue the backdating probes but acknowledge opportunity costs, meaning that other regulatory or enforcement endeavors will have to be sacrificed in order to shift resources to the backdating inquiries.[59]

The agency's investigators are reportedly combing corporate disclosures to identify patterns that suggest that executives consistently exercised their stock options at advantageous share prices, such as a monthly or quarterly low. When such cases trigger suspicions, the investigators may then request brokerage firm records and other documents from the firm to determine whether actual and reported exercise dates are consistent.[60]

At this early juncture in backdating probes, it is uncertain how widespread the abuse has been. Some predict that a relatively small number of firms will be sanctioned. But others are less sanguine about the pervasiveness of the abuse, citing the mounting number of firms that have discovered possible backdating irregularities, and Lie's finding that from 1996 and 2002, 29% of the sampled firms appear to have backdated or otherwise manipulated their option grants. And referencing what they perceive as problematic declines in SEC resources devoted to enforcement, they question the SEC's (and the DOJ's) ability to both adequately and comprehensively undertake the probes.[61]

Assuming that many firms are found to have engaged in backdating, some predict that the SEC and the DOJ may ultimately wind up pursuing a "manageable" number of deterrence-oriented enforcements—and ultimately institute what some call a "voluntary compliance protocol." For example, John Coffee, Jr., a law professor at Columbia University and director of its Center on Corporate Governance, speculates that

> after some deterrent prosecutions are brought ... I think you'll have to see the SEC and DOJ come up with voluntary compliance schemes under which companies can conduct an investigation, publish a report, make a confessional disclosure, install preventive controls and get immunity for doing that. Otherwise the DOJ will be doing these cases for a number of years."[62]

### *Late Filings*

As indicated earlier, the longer option grant award disclosure deadlines that existed before SOX appear to have provided much greater opportunities for backdating. Along with other factors like the end of the bull market that began in the 1990s, SOX's tightened reporting requirements appear to have helped reduce backdating's incidence, giving some SEC officials a sense that the abuse is largely a thing of the past.

However, when grant award disclosures are filed late, greater opportunity exists for the retroactive falsification of grant dates. And in the post-SOX era, there is research that indicates the ongoing presence of a non-trivial level of late filings. For example, after examining several thousand filings, one study found that (despite an SEC website that should have simplified the filing process) 13% of the insider option grant award filings in 2005 were tardy.[63] This finding led the study's authors, who include Erik Lie, the author of the backdating study that helped alert the SEC to the existence of the backdating abuse, to question whether the late filings reflect the existence of continued and widespread backdating.

Research by the proxy advisory firm Glass Lewis & Company, *The Backdating Scandal's Second Act?*, involved combing through hundreds of thousands of executive grant award disclosures between January 2004 to June 2006. In the end, the study found some 6,000 questionably timed stock-options grants to executives that had been tardily filed.[64]

Reflecting on the potential ramifications of their research, analysts at Glass Lewis observed that although they could not definitively ascertain the persistence of backdating from the study, they noted that "given the sheer number of delinquent filings, the supposed method of regulation that was going to close the door on backdating remains ajar.... "[65] Additionally, the analysts said the study raised the prospect that "hundreds" of firms may have either knowingly or accidentally backdated awards after the 2002 changes.[66]

Since August 2002, the SEC has pursued enforcement actions against six delinquent filers, usually as part of larger investigations.[67] Noting that the lateness of the filings creates a greater opportunity for option grant abuse, Glass Lewis' researchers described the agency's enforcement as far too lax and thus lacking in significance as a meaningful deterrent to tardy submissions.[68]

In 2004, the SEC created a unit to pursue delinquent filers but, historically, enforcement against late filers appears to have been viewed as a low priority area with relatively little benefit relative to its costs. In response to the concerns raised by the Glass Lewis study, SEC officials spoke of their intent to continue to monitor whether backdating appears to be linked to delinquent Form 4 filings and to pursue enforcement actions where appropriate.[69] Agency officials also emphasized that late Form 4 filings are most pronounced among smaller firms (with less stringent internal controls) compared to larger firms with market capitalizations of at least $750 million.[70]

### *The Question of the SEC's Alertness to Misconduct*

As indicated earlier, the SEC's interest in the backdating misconduct appears to derive from the work of others, specifically research conducted by University of Iowa Professor Erik Lie. This would appear to be the third time in little more than a decade in which the agency relied on the "gumshoe" work of outsiders to learn of the existence of potentially widespread misconduct among entities that it regulates.

- A series of mid-1990s SEC enforcement actions and Nasdaq regulatory reforms stemmed from academic research that identified price rigging by some Nasdaq market makers.
- In 2003, New York Attorney General Spitzer announced that his office had discovered evidence that major mutual fund companies had been complicit in either illegal or unethical trading schemes, revelations that resulted in widespread probes, money settlements, and the SEC's adoption of a series of fund regulatory reforms.[71]

In the wake of the fund scandals, the SEC implemented a host of internal administrative reforms aimed at improving its alertness to misconduct. Still, when combined with current concerns over the possibility that the agency may face serious resource constraints this latest example of SEC reliance on investigations surfaced by others could be a potential area for oversight.

## POTENTIAL POLICY OPTIONS

Generally expressing their faith in the efficacy of existing regulations and laws (like SOX's two-day option grant reporting requirement) to curb abuse, various officials at federal agencies currently involved in the backdating probes, including the heads of the SEC and the IRS, question the need for additional measures at this point.[72] Yet, while it is almost universally agreed that backdating is no longer the kind of problem that it was several years ago, some research suggests it has been far from eliminated. Given these lingering concerns, this section describes a number of initiatives promoted as ways to help further stem backdating. Possible benefits of a policy option may be weighed against its administrative and compliance costs.

## Improve Enforcement of Timely Filing of Option Awards

Historically, the SEC has reportedly viewed enforcing tardily filed executive grant award disclosures as a low priority, low payoff exercise.[73] From 2001 to 2005, the agency reportedly brought 12 enforcement actions that included charges of late form 4 filings. Agency officials, however, say that it has a program that regularly reviews delinquent filers and brings actions where needed.[74] But late disclosures provide greater opportunities for backdating and critics argue that lax enforcement lowers deterrence, increasing the odds that firms may deliberately backdate.[75]

## Require Same Day Filing of Option Grants

Claiming that backdating could be eliminated by requiring that stock options grants, including exercise prices, be filed electronically with the SEC on the day that they are granted, Professor Lie has argued for the agency to institute such reform.[76] While making the case for the change, he has emphasized that filing is already a simple process, that the forms can be filed online, and that some option grants are already filed on the same day.[77] In research that appears to lend some support to such reform, Professor Lie and co-researcher Randall Heron found that 7.0% of a large sample of grants filed within the two day requirement were backdated,[78] suggesting that the two day filing window has reduced but not totally eliminated the opportunity to backdate option grants.

## Require Scheduling of Grants of Executive Stock Options

Compared to scheduled option grant awards, unscheduled grant awards give executives greater opportunity to take advantage of market vagaries, (or to time awards around the release of positive or negative corporate news). As a consequence, some observers propose that firms only be allowed to issue option grants on a regularly scheduled basis. One criticism of requiring only scheduled option grants is that it would unfairly tie the hands of firms who need to make unscheduled awards due to unexpected contingencies. From a jurisdictional standpoint, this kind of reform is the traditional province of corporate boards, although some observers have suggested that the SEC might have authority to intervene in this area.[79]

## Ban Equity-based Pay for Top Attorneys and Board Members

Some observers have proposed banning the use of equity-based compensation for corporate lawyers and directors. They argue that compared to conventional fixed compensation, equity-based pay is more apt to undermine the officials' roles as gatekeepers/protectors against executive misconduct like backdating. It would be unprecedented for a regulator like the SEC or an exchange in its capacity as an SRO to place limits on certain kinds of corporate pay. But employing similar arguments against compensating directors with equity-based pay, a number of firms are voluntarily deciding not to do so. For example, in October 2006, Campbell Soup announced that starting in 2007, it would stop issuing stock options as part of its directors' compensation. And in December 2006, IBM announced that beginning in 2007, as part of a companywide effort to reduce the reliance on the grants, it would stop granting stock options to its outside directors. Arguments against placing proscriptions on equity-based pay would, however, include the following: (1) there is little empirical evidence linking such the provision of such equity-based pay to improprieties on the part of corporate executives; and (2) there is research that has found a positive correlation between paying directors with stock options and certain measures of corporate financial performance.[80]

## Increase Shareholder Roles in the Election of Board Members

In July 2003, the SEC proposed a rule that under certain conditions would have allowed public company shareholders with more than 5% of a company's voting securities to have their nominees for board membership included in a company's proxy materials.[81] This would enable large investors to formally nominate candidates for the board—a change from the current regime under which board members are almost always nominated by firm executives. A response to widespread concerns over the accountability of corporate directors after a number of corporate scandals, the proposal received the support of various observers, including some institutional investors who argued that the integrity of corporate boards would be enhanced by an expanded shareholder role in the director nomination process. Similarly, it could be argued that such a reform could result in boards being populated with a greater number of outside directors who are less beholden to management and better able to provide independent oversight and scrutiny of executive compensation practices and excesses, including backdating. It also could be argued that the research described earlier—that found that large numbers of outside large directors appear to have been the beneficiaries of options manipulation—provides additional support for such reform.

In August 2006, the United States Court of Appeals for the Second Circuit reached a decision in American Federation of State, County and Municipal Employees Pension Plan v. American International Group, Inc. This ruling was the appeal's courts response to an earlier petition by the American Federation of State, County and Municipal Employees (AFSCME) that the American International Group's (AIG) rejection of its effort to place a binding shareholder proposal in the company's proxy materials that would have changed its bylaws to facilitate shareholder nomination of directors be reversed. Historically, the SEC has allowed firms to exclude shareholder proposals from their proxies, as it did in this case. However, the Second Circuit found the SEC's policy in this area to be inconsistent and asked the agency to clarify it.

The SEC issued a press release saying that the commissioners would be responding to the court decision during an October 2006 meeting, which they did not do. Later, it issued a press release saying that the commissioners would be considering proposals for revisions to its earlier shareholder proxy access initiatives at a meeting on December 13, 2006,[82] which they also did not do.

## Eliminate the Cap on Deduction for Executive Pay

As previously indicated, in 1993, OBRA added Section 162(m) to the Internal Revenue Code, which limited a company's tax deduction on what it pays each of its top executives to $1 million, but exempted "performance-based" pay like stock options. In conjunction with other developments like the bull market of the 1990s and the pressure on firms to provide executive pay that better aligned executives' incentives with the interests of firm investors, OBRA is widely believed to have been a factor in the rise in the use of stock options. Some have argued that rescinding OBRA, or limiting the kinds of exempt performance-based pay could help stem the use of stock options, thus limiting the supply of potentially backdatable stock options.[83] This kind of reform could, however, be criticized for being an exceptionally blunt approach that is only weakly connected to the basic machinery of backdating, raising questions about its ability to help stem the abuse. Moreover, a comprehensive look at OBRA's impact on CEO pay found that given the minimal impact that tax deductibility of executive compensation tends to have on firm profitability, the actual role that OBRA has played on the configuration of CEO pay "remains an open question."[84]

## APPENDIX A. OTHER FORMS OF TIMING MANIPULATION

In addition to backdating, three other types of timing manipulation should be noted.[85] First, *spring-loading* and *bullet-dodging* concern the timing of option grants to coincide with public announcements by the issuing company.[86] *Spring-loading* occurs when stock options are issued in advance of a positive public announcement by the issuing company, which is expected to drive up the market value of the stock. Because the recipients of the stock options knew that the public announcement would be positive, but other investors did not, the recipients of the stock options received a "windfall" gain. *Bullet-dodging* is the reverse of spring-loading. Stock options are issued shortly after a negative public announcement by the company. Investors are surprised by the negative announcement, may overreact, and may temporarily reduce the market value of the stock, at which point the stock options are issued. Subsequently, if the price recovers, recipients of these stock options will have received a favorable exercise price. Spring-loading and bullet-dodging can also be applied to the timing of *option repricing.* When a company's stock price falls significantly below the exercise price of its stock options, some companies reprice the option's exercise price. The justification for repricing stock options is to restore their incentive effect.

Second, the *timing of corporate announcements* can be manipulated in relation to known dates for the granting of options. For example, a high tech firm could delay the announcement of a technological breakthrough until after the date of the granting of stock options.

Third, some executives have *changed the exercise date without disclosure* in order to reduce their tax liability.[87] By backdating the exercise date on their stock options to when the stock price was lower, executives can convert regular income into capital gains, which are taxed at a much lower marginal tax rate.[88]

In some cases more than one form of timing manipulation may occur, and it may be difficult to empirically separate the relative magnitude of these different forms of manipulation.

## APPENDIX B. QUALIFIED STOCK OPTIONS

Two types of stock options qualify for the special tax treatment provided in IRC Section 421: *incentive stock options and employee stock purchase plans*. Both types require that the recipient be an employee of the company (or its parent or subsidiary) from the time the option is granted until at least three months before the option is exercised. The option may cover stock in the company or its parent or subsidiary.

Both types of qualified stock options receive some tax benefit under current law. The employee recognizes no income (for regular tax purposes) when the options are granted or when they are exercised. Taxes (under the regular tax) are not imposed until the stock purchased by the employee is sold. If the stock is sold after it has been held for at least two years from the date the option was granted *and* one year from the date it was exercised, the difference between the market price of the stock when the option was exercised and the price for which it was sold is taxed at long-term capital gains rates. If the option price was less than 100% of the fair market value of the stock when it was granted, the difference between the exercise price and the market price (the discount) is taxed as ordinary income (when the stock is sold).

Companies generally receive no deduction for qualified stock options, so the tax advantage accrues to the employee, not the employer. Companies that would not be taxable anyway, such as start-up companies not yet profitable, would care little (if at all) about the tax deduction and would be expected to use this method of compensation. Many companies that are taxable grant qualified stock options, however, so these options must have some advantage that outweighs the tax cost. In some cases, the companies no doubt find that rewarding their employees with qualified stock options is worth the cost; in other cases, perhaps, the officers and employees who receive the options exercise special influence over the companies' compensation policies.

If the stock is not held for the required two years from the granting of the option and one year from its exercise, special rules apply. The employee is taxed at ordinary income tax rates instead of capital gains rates on the difference between the price paid for the stock and its market value either when the option was exercised or when the stock was sold, whichever is less. The company is then allowed a deduction just as if the employee's taxable gain were ordinary compensation paid in the year the stock is sold.

Imposing the alternative minimum tax on incentive stock options reduces their tax advantage; for persons paying the AMT, the tax treatment is similar to the regular tax treatment of nonqualified options.[89] In some cases, individuals have incurred a significant tax liability from exercising their incentive stock options but had not sold their stock before the price dramatically declined. The alternative minimum tax in combination with other rules could cause a large tax liability that could not be offset with an offsetting loss when the stock price fell.[90] On December 20, 2006, this "unfair" situation was solved by passage of the Tax Relief Act and Health Care Act of 2006 (H.R. 6408), in Section 402.

## Incentive Stock Options

Incentive stock options (IRC Section 422) must be granted in accordance with a written plan approved by the shareholders. The plan must designate the number of shares to be subject to the options and specify the classes of employees eligible to participate in the plan. The options must be exercised within 10 years from the grant date. The market value of the stock for any incentive stock options exercisable in any year is limited to $100,000 for any individual. This is the limit on the amount that receives favorable tax treatment, not on the amount that may be granted; options for stock exceeding $100,000 in market value are treated as nonqualifying options. There are additional restrictions for options granted to persons owning more than 10% of the outstanding stock. The value of incentive stock options is included in minimum taxable income in the year of exercise.

The tax code (IRC Section 422) states that "the option price is not less than the fair market value of the stock at the time such option is granted." But the code (IRC Section 422) also states the this requirement is met if there are "good faith efforts to value stock."

## Employee Stock Purchase Plans

An employee stock purchase plan (IRC Section 423) must also be a written plan approved by the shareholders, but this type of plan must generally cover all full-time employees with at least two years of service (or all except highly compensated employees). It must exclude any employee who owns (or would own after exercising the options) 5% or more of the company's stock. The option price must be at least 85% of the fair market value of the stock either when the option is granted or when it is exercised, whichever is less. The options must be exercised within a limited time (no more than five years). The plan must not allow any employee to accrue rights to purchase more than $25,000 in stock in any year.

# APPENDIX C. LITERATURE ABOUT BACKDATING

Literature about backdating can be divided into academic studies and *Wall Street Journal* (*WSJ*) articles. The academic work provided the statistical verification of the hypothesis of backdating. Initially, the academic work did not specific any particular corporations involved in backdating. Articles in the *Wall Street Journal* named specific corporations that had backdated their stock options. Furthermore, these WSJ articles provided widespread publicity for the backdating issue to both the business community and the general public.

## Academic Studies

### *Erik Lie*

Professor Erik Lie, currently on the faculty of the University of Iowa, initially formulated the hypothesis that some companies, without disclosure, backdated dates for grants of options to times when prices of their stock were low.[91] Dr. Lie wrote an article titled "On the Timing of CEO Stock Options Awards," which included an empirical analysis supporting his backdating hypothesis, and sent a copy of this article to the SEC in 2004.[92] In May 2005, his article was published in *Management Science*.[93]

Dr. Lie indicated that "the board of directors of a company generally assigns the administration of the [stock option] grants of the stock option plan to the compensation committee."[94] Executives, however, may be able to influence the decisions of the committee because executives often propose parameters of stock option grants, executives often have close personal friendships with some committee members, and executives may influence the timing of compensation committee meetings.[95] Using a sample of almost 6,000 stock option grants to chief executive officers (CEOs) between 1981 and 1992, he conducted several statistical analyses and concluded "that the abnormal stock returns are negative before the award dates and positive afterward."[96] These findings were consistent with his hypothesis of backdating of stock options without disclosure. The publication of Dr. Lie's article led to SEC investigations of the timing of the granting of stock options by certain companies.

### *Heron and Lie (article)*

In their forthcoming article in the *Journal of Financial Economics* titled "Does Backdating Explain the Stock Price Patten Around Executive Stock Option Grants?," Professor Randall A. Heron and Professor Erik Lie examined the frequency of backdating of stock options since August 29, 2002, when the Sarbanes-Oxley Act (P.L. 107-204)[97] mandated that the SEC change the reporting regulations for stock option grants.[98] Before the change, executives receiving stock options had up to 45 days after the end of the company's fiscal year to report them to the SEC.[99] After August 29, 2002, recipients of stock options must report them to the SEC within two business days of receiving the grant. One day after receiving this information, the SEC makes it public, and now firms with corporate websites are required to post this information on the day after they disclose it to the SEC. The authors stated that

> if backdating produced the abnormal return patterns around executive option grants, we hypothesize that the new reporting requirements should substantially dampen the abnormal return patterns that previously had been intensifying over time.[100]

Heron and Lie utilized a large sample of stock option grants to CEOs between August 29, 2002, and November 30, 2004, and compared this sample with a large sample from January 1, 2000, to August 28, 2002. The authors concluded that

> Overall, we find evidence suggesting that backdating is the major source of the abnormal stock return patterns around executive stock option grants. Our evidence further suggests that the new reporting requirements have greatly curbed backdating, but have not eliminated it. To eliminate

> backdating, it appears that the requirements need to be tightened further, such that grants have to be reported on the grant day or, at the latest, on the day thereafter. In addition, the SEC naturally has to enforce the requirements.[101]

Thus, the authors found that while the undisclosed backdating of stock options still occurs, it was far more prevalent before new reporting regulations took effect on August 29, 2002.

***Heron and Lie (working paper)***

On July 14, 2006, Professor Randall A. Heron and Professor Erik Lie published a working paper based on a sample of 39,888 stock option grants of 7,774 companies to top executives, which were dated between January 1, 1996 and December 1, 2005.[102] (Top executives consisted of CEOs, Presidents, and Chairmen of the Board.) The authors estimated that before August 29, 2002, when the new two-day filing took effect, 23.0% of unscheduled, at the money stock option grants were backdated.[103] But from August 29, 2002 through December 1, 2005, only an estimated 10.0% of this type of stock option grants were backdated.[104] The authors estimated that 29.2% of the 7,774 companies engaged in timing manipulation for stock option grants to top executives .[105]

## Narayanan and Seyhum

In January 2005, Professors M.P. Narayanan and H. Nejat Seyhun published a University of Michigan working paper titled "Do Managers Influence Their Pay? Evidence from Stock Price Reversals around Executive Option Grants."[106] The authors tested their hypothesis that managers influence the grant date stock price for their stock options. They used a data base of 605,106 option grant filings by insiders between 1992 and 2002. The authors found that the abnormal stock return reversals on the grant date were consistent with the influence hypothesis. They found that "the market-adjusted return for the 90 days preceding the grant date is about—3.6% and the return for the 90 days following the grant date is about 9.4%."[107] The authors concluded that the much smaller absolute value of the return before the grant date than after the grant date suggested that the firms were engaged in behavior that went beyond controlling the timing of the grants and the timing of corporate information disclosures.[108] The authors also advanced the hypothesis "that grant dates are set on a 'back-date' basis, that is in many cases, the lowest stock price during a window is picked as the grant date ex-post."[109] They found statistical evidence that was consistent with their backdating hypothesis.[110]

### *Narayanan, Schipani, and Seyhun*

Professors M.P. Narayanan, Cindy A. Schipani, and H. Nejat Seyhun wrote an article titled "The Economic Impact of Backdating of Executive Stock Options," in the *Michigan Law Review*.[111] They

> discuss four consequences of misdating that can adversely impact shareholder value: 1) Legal issues: There are legal consequences arising from backdating or forward-dating without complete disclosure. In addition, the ethical issues raised might have economic consequences as they undermine the investors' confidence in the top executives; 2) Tax issues: The tax treatment of in-the-money options with implications for both the company and its executives; 3) Corporate disclosure issues: Disclosure of misdating practices can lead to restatement of earnings as the camouflaged pay is recognized as compensation expense. The reduced earnings can result in a downward reassessment of shareholder value; and 4) Incentive issues: Misdating amounts to stealth compensation. If this is done because executives have captured the compensation process, then the managers are being inefficiently compensated, resulting in incorrect incentives.[112]

The authors computed that the upper bound of the average benefit from potential backdating was $3 million for executives based on a sample of 39,864 option grants from 43 firms listed on a *Wall Street Journal website*.[113] In comparison, these firms experienced an average loss of $510 million in the value of their outstanding stock as a result of being implicated in backdating of stock options.[114]

### *Bebchuk, Grinstein, and Peyer (Lucky CEOs)*

Professors Lucian Bebchuk, Yaniv Grinstein, and Urs Peyer, examined what they called "lucky" grants, which they defined at stock option grants given at the lowest price of the stock during the month.[115] They found that during the period 1996-2005, about 1,150 lucky grants to 850 CEOs (about 10% of all CEOs) and provided by about 720 firms (about 12% of all firms) involved opportunistic timing, primarily backdating.[116] The percentage of "lucky grants" declined from 15% before SOX to 8% after SOX.[117]

The authors identified links between the manipulation of the timing of granting stock options and business governance. The authors stated that

> Lucky grants are more likely to occur when the firm lacks a majority of independent directors and when the CEO has longer tenure, both factors associated with greater CEO influence on the company's pay-setting and governance processes. Relatedly, we [the authors] find that CEOs receiving lucky grants also receive total compensation from other sources that is higher relative to peer firms, thus finding no evidence that extra gains from grant timing manipulation was used by firms as a substitute for other compensation forms.[118]

The authors also found links between the manipulation of the timing of stock options and the potential gains from this manipulation.

> Not only is manipulation more common in firms with higher stock price volatility, but it is also more likely to occur, for a given CEO and firm, in months in which the potential gain from it is higher relative to other times. Our analysis also highlights the existence of serial luck. Luck is persistent with CEOs more likely being lucky in their next grant when their prior grant was lucky.[119]

Finally, the authors concluded that "by providing estimates of the substantial incidence of lucky grants, firms, and CEOs in old economy firms, ... [their] analysis dispels the impression that grant manipulation is concentrated in new economy firms."[120]

### *Bebchuk, Grinstein, and Peyer (Lucky Directors)*

Professors Lucian Bebchuk, Yaniv Grinstein, and Urs Peyer analyzed whether or not outside directors received option grants involving opportunistic timing; that is, timing manipulation. Their sample consisted of "all grants given to directors of the about 6,000 public companies in the Thompson database during the decade of 1996-2005."[121] The authors found that 804 grant events during this period were due to opportunistic timing rather than mere luck, and 457 firms (7.1% of all firms) were involved.[122] The percentage of these lucky grant events was 35.7% before SOX and 25.4% after SOX.[123] An estimated 1,389 directors (or 4.6% of all directors) received one or more opportunistically timed grants.[124] Several statistical tests were consistent with the hypothesis that backdating played a significant role in opportunistic timing grants of options that benefitted directors.[125] The authors acknowledge that their methodology does not measure timing manipulation of stock options that occurred in "small look-back periods."[126] In contrast, some other studies measure all timing manipulation of options regardless of the time period.

Furthermore, the authors state that their analysis "does not show what role, if any, outside directors played in the opportunistic timing of their own grants."[127]

### *Bernile, Jarrell, and Mulcahey*

Professor Gennaro Bernile, Professor Gregg Jarrell, and Howard Mulcahey analyzed the effect of the options backdating scandal on the stock-price performance of 110 companies.[128] They examined the stock prices of 110 companies involved in the options backdating scandal that were named on a web page posted by *the Wall Street Journal*. The authors estimated that the cumulative abnormal return for these 110 companies over a period of 140 trading days was negative 25.86%, which equaled a loss in the value of stock of over $100 billion. These 140 trading days consisted of 60 days before and 80 days after the first company disclosure about option-backdating. For the period of May 16, 2005 through November 15, 2006 (100 trading days before and 380 trading days after Erik Lie's initial backdating article), the authors calculated a cumulative abnormal return for the companies of negative 54.14%, which equaled a loss in the value of stock of approximately $250 billion.

### *Wall Street Journal Articles*

Dr. Lie's articles did not mention any company by name, but his hypothesis of backdating of stock options without disclosure was tested for five corporations by Charles Forelle and James Bandler and reported in an article in *The Wall Street Journal* on March 18, 2006.[129] These authors examined the timing of stock option grants for five corporations. In each case, stock options were granted on dates when prices were extremely low. The authors concluded that the likelihood of this "happening by chance was extraordinarily remote."[130] For example, one CEO received six stock-option grants from 1995 to 2002, which occurred at dates when the stock price was unusually low.[131] The author found that the probability of these dates being selected by chance was around one in 300 billion.

On May 22, 2006, Charles Forelle and James Bankler wrote a second article in *The Wall Street Journal* concerning backdating of stock options without disclosure.[132] The authors identified five more companies "with highly improbable patterns of options grants."[133]

# Appendix D. Literature about Other Types of Timing Manipulation

This appendix briefly summarizes several significant studies of other forms of the timing of stock options.

## Yermack (Spring-Loading)

Professor David Yermack wrote the first article concerning the manipulation of the timing of stock options.[134] He formulated the hypothesis that some CEOs arranged for the award of the stock option to occur shortly before public announcements of positive information about their companies. This concept was later called spring-loading. In order to test his hypothesis, he used a sample of 620 stock option awards to CEOs of Fortune 500 companies between 1992 and 1994. At a 1% level of significance, he found that the average abnormal increase in option award value was $30,000 after 20 trading days and $48,900 after 50 trading days.[135]

## Chauvin and Shenoy (Manipulation of Information Flow)

Professors Keith W. Chauvin and Catherine Shenoy analyzed abnormal stock price decreases prior to executive stock option grants.136 They developed the hypothesis that executives cause bad news to be released prior to the time that options are granted in order to set the strike price of the options at a lower level. This negative information could be in the form of a formal public announcement, or else insiders "can put a more negative 'spin' on information than otherwise, speak 'off the record' to analysts, or strategically use rumor and innuendo to 'leak' information." The authors statistically analyzed a sample of 783 stock option grants from May 1991 to February 1994 issued to 209 CEOs and found "a significant stock price decrease prior to executive stock option grants."137

## Aboody and Kasznik (Manipulation of Information Flow)

Professors David Aboody and Ron Kasznik investigated their hypothesis "that CEOs manage investors' expectations around fixed dates of scheduled awards for their stock options by delaying good news and rushing forward bad news.[138] The authors tested their hypothesis by using a sample of 2,039 stock option awards made between 1992 and 1996 to the CEOs of 572 firms."[139] The authors concluded that "overall, our findings provide evidence that CEOs of firms with scheduled awards make opportunistic voluntary disclosures that maximize their stock option compensation."[140]

## Callaghan, Saly, and Subramaniam (Timing of Repricing)

Professors Sandra Renfro Callaghan, P. Jane Saly, and Chandra Subramaniam investigated the hypothesis that executive stock option repricings were systematically timed to coincide with favorable movements in the company's stock price.[141] If the exercise price of the stock options falls well below the market price of the stock, some executives maintain that the stock options should be repriced in order to "retain valued employees and to restore incentives."[142] The authors used a sample of 236 repricing of options for 166 companies from the period 1992 through 1997.[143] Their statistical analysis suggested that managers opportunistically timed repricings in conjunction with the release of corporate news.[144] Executives who anticipated favorable earnings reports repriced their option prior to the public announcement of the report. Conversely, executives who anticipated negative earnings reports repriced their options after the public release of earnings.

## End Notes

[1] Eric Dash, "Dodging Taxes Is a New Stock Options Scheme," *New York Times*, Oct. 30, 2006, p. 1.

[2] Although numerous empirical studies have found statistical support for the hypothesis that corporate executives and directors have benefitted from the undisclosed backdating of stock options, this does not prove that a particular corporate official was responsible or even knowledgeable of the backdating.

[3] Stephen J. Crimmins, "Sorting Out the Cases Involving Backdating of Stock Option," Viewpoint in *Daily Tax Report*, no. 232, Dec. 4, 2006, p. J1.

[4] Andrew Osterland, "SEC Halves Backdating Backlog," *Financial Week*, Dec. 12, 2007.

[5] For a list and status of 140 of these companies (last updated on Sept. 4, 2007), see the *Wall Street Journal* online site at http://online.wsj.com/public/resources visited Jan. 30, 2009.

[6] Therese Poletti, "Buck Stops Here Rhetoric Doesn't Wash," *Market Watch*, Dec. 13, 2007.

[7] Brocade CEO Reyes Gets 21 Months Following Verdict on Options Backdating, *Daily Tax Report*, no. 11, Jan. 17, 2008, p. K2.

[8] "Former UnitedHealth CEO McGuire to Pay Record $468 Million for Options Backdating," *Daily Report for Executives*, no. 235, Dec. 7, 2007, p. K4.

[9] Ibid.

[10] U.S. Securities and Exchange Commission, *Spotlight On Stock Options Backdating*, pp. 1-5. Available at http://www.sec.gov/spotlight/optionsbackdating.htm, visited Jan. 30, 2009.

[11] Members of the company's compensation committee are responsible for determining the CEO's compensation including grants of stock options. But some CEOs have simply set their own grants of stock options or have "influenced" members of the compensation committee to grant them their desired level of stock options.

[12] Nonqualified options are defined in the next section of this chapter.

[13] Nonqualified options are not guaranteed; that is, they have no value if the company goes bankrupt.

[14] A detailed description of qualified stock options is presented in **Appendix B**.

[15] U.S. Congress, House Committee on the Budget, *Omnibus Budget Reconciliation Act of 1993*, report to accompany H.R. 2264, 103rd Cong., 1st sess., H.Rept. 103-111, (Washington: GPO, 1993), p. 635.

[16] For historical data on individual income tax rates, see CRS Report RL34498, *Statutory Individual Income Tax Rates and Other Elements of the Tax System: 1988 through 2009*, by Maxim Shvedov.

[17] H.Rept. 103-111, p. 646.

[18] IRS Code Sec. 162(m), (4)(C).

[19] A National Bureau of Economic Research (NBER) study found that section 162(m) had no significant effects on overall executive compensation because of the exemption from the cap of performance-based compensation, the ability to defer compensation, and the cap only applying to salaries of five executives. For these results, see Nancy L. Rose and Catherine Wolfram, "Regulating Executive Pay: Using the Tax Code to Influence CEO Compensation," NBER Working Paper 7842, Cambridge, Mass.: National Bureau of Economic Research, Aug. 2000, 47 p.

[20] "Grassley Takes Aim at Stock Options Backdating, Executive Pay," *Press Release from Senator Grassley's Office*, Sept. 6, 2006.

[21] "Testimony Concerning Options Backdating by Christopher Cox, Chairman, U.S. Securities and Exchange Commission Before the U.S. Senate Committee on Banking, Housing and Urban Affairs," Sept. 6, 2006.

[22] JoAnn S. Lublin and Scott Thurm, "Behind Soaring Executive Pay, Decades of Failed Restraints," *Wall Street Journal*, Oct. 12, 2006, p. A16.

[23] In 2004, FASB adopted a controversial accounting rule, FAS 123(R), which requires public companies to incorporate the estimated value of their option grants as a cost in their financial disclosures. For most firms, the requirement went into effect for fiscal years after June 15, 2005. One study found that after the accounting change, firms appear to have reduced their level of executive option grants, replacing them with other forms of compensation. Mary Carter, Luann Lynch, and A. Irem Tuna, "The Role of Accounting in the Design of CEO Equity Compensation," *The Accounting Review*, March 2007.

[24] Corporate executives involved in undisclosed backdating of their stock options may lose their jobs, may have to pay substantial penalties for violating tax and securities laws, and also risk incarceration. In addition, these executives must bear high costs of litigation. The executives who have engaged in undisclosed backdating have violated SEC's disclosure rules, accounting rules, and tax laws.

[25] Gennaro Bernile, Gregg A. Jarrell, and Howard Mulcahey, "The Effect of the Options Backdating Scandal on the Stock-Price Performance of 110 Accused Companies," Simon School of Business, University of Rochester, Working Paper No. FR06-10, p. 11. Available at http://ssrn.com/abstract=952524, visited Feb. 2, 2009.

[26] While New York Stock Exchange (NYSE) bylaws mandate a delisting when annual reports are not provided on time, the Nasdaq (where the vast majority of firms with backdating concerns are listed) can delist when there is a late quarterly report. A delisting also results in fiscal pain to the exchange since it is forced to forego the listing fees that the firms pay them. In 2006, companies listed on the Nasdaq paid an annual fee of $75,000 if they had total shares outstanding of over 150 million. In 2007, this fee was raised to $95,000. Current data on the Nasdaq fee structure for listing is available at http://www.nasdaq.com/about/nasdaq_listing_req_fees.pdf, visited Feb. 3, 2009.

[27] The general convention is that at the end of an internal probe, a firm is expected to provide its findings to federal prosecutors who use the information to determine whether to pursue the case further. Historically, providing such self-investigated findings has often resulted in federal agencies showing greater leniency in the punishment that they mete out to offending firms. James Bandler and Kara Scannell, "Legal Aid: In Options Probes, Private Law Firms Play Crucial Role; As More than 130 Companies Come Under Scrutiny, Government Relies on Help; Questions about Fairness," *Wall Street Journal*, Oct. 28, 2006, p. A1.

[28] Anne Tergesen, "Those Options Could Cost You," *Business Week*, Oct. 2, 2006, p. 96.

[29] On Feb. 8, 2007, the IRS announced it would provide penalty and interest relief to workers who unwittingly exercised backdated and other mispriced stock options in 2006, but the compliance initiative did not extend to company executives or other insiders who benefitted most from the schemes. Internal Revenue Service, *IRS Offers Opportunity for Employers to Satisfy Tax Obligations of Rank-and-File Employees with 'Backdated' Stock Options*, IRS News Release, IR-2007-30, Feb. 8, 2007, p. 1.

[30] Tergesen, p. 96.

[31] Ibid.

[32] Erik Lie, Testimony before the U.S. Senate Committee on Banking, Housing, and Urban Affairs, Sept. 6, 2006, p. 1.

[33] Joni L. Andrioff, "Deferred Compensation Revolution—Tough Transition to a Statutory System," *Taxes: The Tax Magazine*, vol. 83, no. 5, May 2005, p. 65.

[34] Ibid., p. 66.

[35] Internal Revenue Service, "Interim Guidance on the Application of Section 409A to Accelerated Payments to Satisfy Federal Conflict of Interest Requirements," *Internal Revenue Bulletin*, 2006-29, July 17, 2006, p. 1. Available at http://www.irs.gov/irb/2006-29_IRB/ar11.html.

[36] Financial Accounting Standards Board, "FASB Issues Final Statement on Accounting for Share-Based Payment," *FASB News Release*, Dec.16, 2004.

[37] Mary Ellen Carter, Luann Lynch, and A. Irem Tuna, "The Role of Accounting in the Design of CEO Equity Compensation," *The Accounting Review*, March 2007.

[38] See CRS Report RS22583, *Executive Compensation: SEC Regulations and Congressional Proposals*, by Michael V. Seitzinger.

[39] These new rules are stated in 17 CFR Parts 228, 229, et al., pp. 53,158-53,166.

[40] "SEC Votes to Adopt Changes to Disclosure Requirements Concerning Executive Compensation and Related Matters," SEC Press Release 2006-123, July 26, 2006.

[41] "Testimony Concerning Options Backdating by Christopher Cox, SEC Chairman, Before the U.S. Senate Committee on Banking, Housing, and Urban Affairs," Sept. 6, 2006, p.1.

[42] For example, see "Options Backdating: The Enforcement Perspective," Speech by Linda Chatman Thomsen, Director, Division of Enforcement, SEC, Oct. 30, 2006.

[43] For example, see Lucien Bebchuk, Yaniv Grinstein, and Urs Peyer, "Lucky CEOs," Harvard Law School Working Paper, 2006. Available at *http://www.law* and M.P. Narayanan, P.

Seyhun, and Hasan Nejat, "The Dating Game: Do Managers Designate Option Grant Dates to Increase Their Compensation?" 2006. Available at http://ssrn.com/abstract=896164.

[44] David Cho and Carrie Johnson, "Executive-Pay Summaries Conceal as They Reveal," *Washington Post*, Feb. 16, 2007, pp. D1, D2.

[45] Ibid., p. D2.

[46] Ibid.

[47] For example, SEC Commissioner Roel Campos has said that if the evidence was there, he would not be surprised to see a number of enforcement actions against non-managerial directors. "How to be an Effective Board Member," Speech before the HACR Program on Corporate Responsibility, Aug. 15, 2006.

[48] Lucien Bebchuk, Yaniv Grinstein, and Urs Peyer, "Lucky Directors."

[49] Ibid. (Since 2004, firms listed on the NYSE and NASDAQ have been required to have a majority of outside directors.)

[50] Lucien Bebchuk, Yaniv Grinstein, and Urs Peyer, "Lucky CEOs," Harvard Law School Working Paper, Nov. 2006. Available at http://www.law

[51] Ibid.

[52] For a list of corporate officials who have come under scrutiny for past stock-option grants, see http://online.wsj.com/public/resources/documents/info-optionsscore06-exec.html, visited Jan. 2, 2008.

[53] A related concern is that for some companies, abusive or inadvertent backdating could also be symptomatic of inadequate internal controls over accounting procedures. The controversial Section 404 of the Sarbanes Oxley Act of 2002 requires management to assess and publicly report on the effectiveness of a company's internal controls. The requirement has been particularly criticized by smaller publicly traded companies for its costs. See CRS Report RS22482, *Section 404 of the Sarbanes-Oxley Act of 2002 (Management Assessment of Internal Controls): Current Regulation and Congressional Concerns*, by Michael V. Seitzinger.

[54] Concerns that compromised outside accountant integrity may have contributed to the implosion of firms like WorldCom and Enron led to a number of provisions in the Sarbanes Oxley Act of 2002. Among other things, the provisions mandate that corporate audit committees: (1) be composed entirely of independent (non-management) directors, (2) receive information about accounting policies and problems directly from the outside auditor, (3) approve any consulting or non-audit services provided by the auditor to the corporation, and (4) include at least one director who qualifies as a "financial expert."

[55] Some observers claim that some accounting firms have admitted that historically, they have tended to take client firm options documents at "face value." See The Statement of Kurt Schacht Managing Director, Centre for Financial Market Integrity, Chartered Financial Analyst (CFA) Institute Committee on Senate Banking, Housing and Urban Affairs, Sept. 6, 2006.

[56] Erik Lie, and Randy Heron, "Does Backdating Explain the Stock Price Pattern Around Executive Stock Option Grants?" Available at SSRN at http://ssrn.com/abstract.

[57] Scheduled grant awards are awarded during the same time each year, in contrast to unscheduled awards.

[58] "U.S. Senator Richard Shelby Holds a Hearing on Stock Options Backdating, *The Political/Congressional Transcript Wire*, Sept. 8, 2006.

[59] Ibid.

[60] Eric Dash, "Dodging Taxes Is a New Wrinkle in the Stock Options Game," *New York Times*, Oct. 30, 2006, p. C-2.

[61] The agency has also been criticized for the fact that in FY2006 it brought 574 enforcement actions, which represents the lowest number since 2001 and a nearly 9% decrease from FY2005. SEC officials largely attributed this to reversible short-term budgetary and human resource shortfalls. Some observers also note that the 128 agency enforcement actions involving financial disclosure and reporting declined by nearly 31% from FY2005 and are

at their lowest point since 2001, which suggests that SOX has helped instill greater discipline in the way that firms evaluate their internal controls, resulting in fewer financial disclosure and reporting problems. Jack Ciesielski, "SEC Enforcement: Quality Or Quantity?" *The AAO Weblog Delivered by Newstex,* Nov. 6, 2006.

[62] Carolyn Said, "Backdating Issue Moves to Forefront," *San Francisco Chronicle*, July 22, 2006.

[63] Randall Heron and Erik Lie, "What Fraction of Stock Option Grants to Top Executives have Been Backdated or Manipulated?" *University of Iowa School of Business Working Paper*, July 2006. http://www.biz.uiowa.edu/faculty/ elie/Grants-1 1-01-2006.pdf.

[64] As reported in: Therese Poletti, "Silicon Image Prompted to Review Stock Option Grants," *The San Jose Mercury News.com*, Oct. 31, 2006.

[65] Ibid.

[66] Emily Chasan, "Stock Option Backdating Scandal Could Grow," *Reuters*, Oct. 29, 2006.

[67] Emily Chasan, "US SEC Pursued Few Late Stock-Option Filing Issues," *Reuters*, Oct. 30, 2006.

[68] Tiffany Kary and Kaja Whitehouse, "Late Form 4s May Suggest Backdating Continued After SOX," *Dow Jones Newswires*, Oct. 31, 2006.

[69] Form 4 is a "Statement of Changes in Beneficial Ownership of Securities." Information on this form discloses the transactions and holdings of directors, officers, and beneficial owners of registered companies. Additional information about form 4 is available at http://www.sec.gov/about/forms/form4data.pdf, visited Feb. 3, 2009.

[70] Ibid, and Jessica Guynn, "Late Options Filings Proliferate Firm Says," *San Francisco Chronicle*, Oct. 31, 2006, p. D-1.

[71] Prior to Sept. 2003, SEC staffers reportedly did not look for such fund trading abuses because agency officials tended to view other fund actions as higher risk concerns. Agency officials also reportedly believed that mutual funds had internal financial incentives to control frequent and potentially trading because it could lower their returns. But a 2005, Government Accountability Office (GAO) report concluded that SEC inspectors should have detected the market timing abuses before Sept. 2003, when regulators began an industry wide crackdown after New York Attorney General Eliot Spitzer exposed the violations. GAO Report-05313, *Mutual Fund Trading Abuses. Lessons Can be Learned From the SEC Not Having Detected Violations at an Earlier Stage*, April 2005.

[72] For example, see "The Testimony Concerning Options Backdating by Christopher Cox Chairman, SEC, Before the U.S. Senate Committee on Banking, Housing and Urban Affairs," Sept. 6, 2006.

[73] Emily Chasan, "US SEC Pursued Few Late Stock-Option Filing Issues."

[74] Tiffany Kary and Kaja Whitehouse, "Late Form 4s May Suggest Backdating Continued After SOX," Oct. 31, 2006, *Dow Jones Newswires online.*

[75] For example, see "Testimony of Erik Lie Associate Professor of Finance Henry B. Tippie College of Business University of Iowa Before the U.S. Senate Committee on Banking, Housing, and Urban Affairs," Sept. 6, 2006.

[76] Erik Lie, Testimony before the U.S. Senate Committee on Banking, Housing, and Urban Affairs, Sept. 6, 2006, p. 6.

[77] Ibid.

[78] Heron and Lie, "What Fraction of Stock Option Grants to Top Executives have Been Backdated or Manipulated?" p. 3.

[79] For example, see John C. Coffee Jr., "The Dating Game," *The National Law Journal online*, Sept. 4, 2006.

[80] For example, see Eliezer M. Fich and Anil Shivdasani, "The Impact of Stock-Option Compensation for Outside Directors on Firm Value," *The Journal of Business*, vol. 78, 2005, pp. 2,229-2,254.

[81] "Proposed Rule: Security Holder Director Nominations, Release nos. 34-48626; IC-26206; FILE NO. S7-19-03, Securities and Exchange Commission," Oct. 17, 2003.

http://72.14.209.104/ search?q=cache:S2ZazKrK5RIJ:www.sec.gov/rules/proposed/34-48626.htm+sec+and+security+holder+director+nominations&hl=en&ct=clnk&cd=2&gl=us . At least one of two things would have had to have taken place in the previous year's board election to trigger the requirement: (1) 35% or more of shareholders voted to withhold support for at least one director at the company's annual meeting; or (2) a stockholder or a group of shareholders with at least 1% of the company's stock put a proposal on the proxy statement seeking the right to nominate a director, and the proposal was approved by a majority vote.

[82] "Remarks Before the Willamette Securities Regulation Institute by SEC Commissioner Roel Campos," Oct. 19, 2006.

[83] Senate Finance Chairman Max Baucus and ranking committee member Charles Grassley have both reportedly suggested that OBRA may have helped engender the current backdating problems, and have expressed their interest in possibly limiting it. Marie Leone, "Grassley Targets Backdating Advisors," *CFO.com*, Sept. 7, 2006.

[84] Nancy L. Rose, and Catherine Wolfram, "Has the 'Million-Dollar Cap' Affected CEO Pay?" *American Economic Review*, vol. 90, no. 2, May 2000, pp. 197-202.

[85] Whether or not the first two forms of timing manipulation are illegal has not been determined by the SEC or the federal courts.

[86] The SEC has not decided whether or not to pursue cases of spring-loading and bullet-dodging. Rachel McTague, "More Stock-Options Backdating Cases Expected in Near Future, SEC Officials Says," p. A9.

[87] Dash, "Dodging Taxes Is a New Stock Options Scheme," p. 1.

[88] Mark Maremont and Charles Forelle, "How Backdating Helped Executives Cut Their Taxes,*Wall Street Journal,* Dec. 12, 2006, pp. A1, A13.

[89] For a description of the alternative minimum tax, see CRS Report RL30149, *The Alternative Minimum Tax for Individuals*, by Steven Maguire.

[90] For a full explanation of this issue, see CRS Report RS20874, *Taxes and Incentive Stock Options*, by Jane G. Gravelle.

[91] Steve Stecklow, "Options Study Becomes Required Reading," *Wall Street Journal*, May 30, 2006, p. B 1.

[92] Ibid.

[93] Erik Lie, "On the Timing of CEO Stock Option Awards," *Management Science*, vol. 51, no. 5, May 2005, pp. 802- 812.

[94] Ibid., p. 803.

[95] Ibid.

[96] Ibid., p. 810.

[97] The Sarbanes-Oxley Act was passed on July 30, 2002.

[98] Randall A. Heron and Erik Lie, "Does Backdating Explain the Stock Price Pattern Around Executive Stock Option Grants?," *Journal of Financial Economics*, vol. 83, no. 2, pp. 2-3. This article is available at http://www.biz.uiowa.edu/ faculty/elie/GrantsJFE.pdf, visited Jan. 2, 2008.

[99] Ibid., p. 3.

[100] Ibid., p. 3.

[101] Ibid., p. 30.

[102] Heron and Lie, "What Fraction of Stock Option Grants to Top Executives Have Been Backdated or Manipulated?", Working Paper, College of Business, Univ. of Iowa, pp. 4-5.

[103] Ibid., p. 13.

[104] Ibid.

[105] Ibid., p. 4.

[106] M.P. Narayanan and H. Nejat Seyhun, "Do Managers Influence Their Pay? Evidence from Stock Price Reversals around Executive Option Grants," Working Paper No. 927, Ross School of Business, University of Michigan, Jan. 2005, 52 p.

[107] Ibid., p. 30.

[108] Ibid., pp. 25-24.
[109] Ibid., p. 4.
[110] Ibid., pp. 25-27.
[111] M.P. Narayanan, Cindy A. Schipani, and H. Nejat Seyhun, "The Economic Impact of Backdating of Executive Stock Options, *Michigan Law Review*, June 2007, available at SSRN: http://ssrn.com/abstract=931889.
[112] Ibid., p. 4.
[113] Ibid., p. 40
[114] Ibid., p. 48.
[115] Lucian Bebchuk, Yaniv Grinstein, and Urs Peyer, "Lucky CEOs," Working Paper, Harvard Law School, Last revision: Nov. 16, 2006, 55 p. Available at http://www.law
[116] Ibid., p. 2.
[117] Ibid., p. 36.
[118] Ibid., p. 35.
[119] Ibid, p. 36.
[120] Ibid., p. 36.
[121] Bebchuk, Grinstein, and Peyer, "Lucky Directors," p. 3.
[122] Ibid., pp. 15-16.
[123] Ibid., p. 15.
[124] Ibid., p. 16.
[125] Ibid., p. 19.
[126] Ibid., p. 7.
[127] Ibid., p. 8.
[128] Gennaro Bernile, Gregg Jarrell, and Howard Mulcahey, "The Effect of the Options Backdating Scandal on the Stock-Price Performance of 110 Accused Companies," Working Paper, Simon School at Univ. of Rochester, Dec. 21, 2006, 18 p. Available at http://papers.ssrn.com/sol3/papers.cfm?abstract_id
[129] Charles Forelle and James Bandler, "The Perfect Payday; Some CEOs Reap Millions by Landing Stock Options When They Are Most Valuable; Luck—or Something Else?," *Wall Street Journal*, March 18, 2006, p. A1.
[130] Ibid.
[131] Ibid.
[132] Charles Forelle and James Bandler, "Matter of Timing: Five More Companies Show Questionable Options Pattern—Chip Industry's KLA-Tencor Among Firms with Grants before Stock-Price Jumps—A 20 Million-to-One Shot," May 22, 2006, p. A1.
[133] Ibid.
[134] David Yermack, "Good Timing: CEO Stock Option Awards and Company News Announcements," *Journal of Finance*, vol. 52, no. 2, June 1997, pp. 449-476.
[135] Ibid., p. 458.
[136] Keith W. Chauvin and Catherine Shenoy, "Stock Price Decreases Prior to Executive Stock Option Grants," *Journal of Corporate Finance*, vol.7, no. 1, March 2001, pp. 53-76.
[137] Ibid., p. 74.
[138] David Aboody and Ron Kasznik, "CEO Stock Awards and the Timing of Corporate Voluntary Disclosures," *Journal of Accounting and Economics*, vol. 29, no. 1, Feb. 2000, pp. 73-100.
[139] Ibid., pp. 73-74.
[140] Ibid., p. 98.
[141] Sandra Renfro Callaghan, P. Jane Saly, and Chandra Subramaniam, "The Timing of Option Repricing," *Journal of Finance*, vol. 59, no. 4, Aug. 2004, pp. 1,651-1,676.
[142] Ibid., p. 1,651.
[143] Ibid., p. 1,654.
[144] Ibid., p. 1,674.

In: Backdating of Stock Options
Editor: Bernard T. Weinstein
ISBN: 978-1-60741-984-6


*Chapter 2*

# OPTIONS BACKDATING: THE ENFORCEMENT PERSPECTIVE*

## *United States Securities and Exchange Commission*

Good afternoon. Thank you so much for spending time today on this important topic. I thought I'd talk a little about where we are from an Enforcement perspective. Looking backward, I'll ruminate a little about how we got here, and finally, at the risk of appearing to be or worse, actually being the secular equivalent of a sanctimonious twit, offer some thoughts looking forward on lessons we might take away from all of this. I should begin of course where I always do—with a disclaimer. My views are my own and do not necessarily reflect the views of the Commission or any other member of the staff. That's the official disclaimer. I have an additional, more personal disclaimer. My views are affected by my view. I have reached the point in life where I view the world through ridiculously expensive progressive lenses, but I guarantee you these lenses are not rose-colored.

So where are we? To recap much of what you may already have read or heard, the Division of Enforcement is investigating over 100 matters relating to potential abuses of employee stock options. The investigations are being conducted by SEC offices throughout the country and are being centrally coordinated and tracked here in Washington. In addition to our investigations,

* This is an edited, reformatted and augmented version of a U. S. Securities and Exchange Commission publication dated October 2006.

there is substantial criminal interest in options matters from United States Attorneys' Offices nationwide. In recent months, the SEC has brought two enforcement actions — one relating to Brocade and another involving Comverse. With respect to both, there are pending parallel criminal actions as well.

As most of you know, the Comverse criminal case has had a certain amount of drama surrounding former CEO Kobi Alexander, who was first a fugitive from justice, and later was located after he took up residence in Namibia, where he is presently fighting extradition to the United States. Taking a very different tack, Comverse's former CFO, David Kreinberg, last week became the first top level executive to settle actions brought by the SEC and the US Attorneys' Office since options backdating came into the media spotlight last Spring. In settling with the SEC, the former Comverse CFO consented to, among other sanctions, a permanent injunction against violation of the securities laws, a permanent bar against serving as a corporate officer or director, and payment of $2.4 million in disgorgement and pre-judgment interest. At the same time, in a related criminal action brought by the US Attorney, Kreinberg pled guilty to securities fraud and conspiracy to commit securities fraud, mail fraud and wire fraud, and he now faces up to 15 years in jail, mandatory restitution and a possible criminal fine.

Despite all the recent media attention, Brocade and Comverse are not the SEC's first stock options cases. In the past few years, we brought two other cases involving option issues in the context of allegations relating to broader financial frauds—one in 2003 involving Peregrine and one in 2004 involving Symbol Technologies. We do not expect to bring 100 enforcement cases regarding stock options—we are focusing on the worst conduct. But we do expect to bring more cases.

To be a little less enforcement-centric, I would also like to talk about where the Commission as a whole is on stock option matters. In addition to the enforcement efforts, others at the Commission have taken two other major steps to address this issue. First, there are the recently adopted rules relating to executive compensation disclosure which specifically address options. These rules, in combination with the prescient provisions of Sarbanes-Oxley requiring timely reporting of stock option grants, will go a very long way toward preventing the kinds of problems we are seeing today from occurring to the same degree in the future. Second, in September the Office of the Chief Accountant issued guidance for companies trying to cope with the financial reporting ramifications of their various historical options practices from a reporting perspective. From my perspective, the collective efforts by the SEC are a model way of addressing an issue—proceeding from various perspectives to come up with practical and wide-ranging solutions.

How did we get here? I'd like to address this on two fronts—first, I'll discuss how we got to our efforts at the Commission and then I'd like to step even further back and talk about some of my impressions on how we ended up with the option issues we are confronting. First, on the SEC front, our investigations are born of a conscious effort to proactively think about where problems might be, to methodically inquire whether there actually are problems, and then to pursue the best ways to address any problems that exist. In this regard, we identified stock options grants as a potential trouble spot several years ago—well ahead of the curve. We examined the academic literature that quantified the potential issues. Our Office of Economic Analysis then analyzed data and refined the areas of concern. And in the Enforcement Division, we gathered information and data regarding specific cases to bring the issues into focus, culminating in our enforcement actions over the last several years.

On a broader plane, how did we get here? I am old enough to remember employee stock options as an anti-takeover device. At that time, in the eighties and nineties, stock options, often in the money, were granted to employees in the hope that a highly-motivated employee pool would put the company in a better position to resist in hostile takeover battles. Over time, shareholders objected to the fact that the options were granted in the money and eventually many companies developed stock option plans in which grants could only be made at the money—that is, at the closing price of the stock on the day of the grant.

Meanwhile other legal and regulatory developments occurred that created distinctions between in the money and at the money options. These developments also tended to favor at the money grants. For example, at the money options received more favorable accounting treatment—they did not need to be expensed. They also generally received more favorable tax treatment. At the money options and other forms of performance-based compensation became even more attractive when the $1 million salary deductibility cap was enacted. So, from the shareholder, accounting and tax perspectives, at the money options had certain distinct advantages.

On the other hand, companies could make in the money grants. While they offended corporate shareholders, had to be expensed by the corporation, and had less favorable tax consequences, they had other advantages. In the money grants offered instant paper gains and the prospect of future wealth that was obviously attractive to employees, some of whom were themselves entrusted to decide precisely when options would be granted. In the late 1990s, companies were facing intense competition to hire and retain the best and brightest employees. At the same time, there was sharp rise in the overall level of executive compensation (some would say astronomical), despite the million-dollar salary deductibility cap. In this environment, cash-strapped companies found stock options an attractive way to provide competitive compensation without further tapping their limited cash flows.

Corporations faced pressures in two different directions—they wanted to attract and retain employees with attractive stock ownership opportunities offered by in the money grants, but they also wanted all the corporate advantages of making at the money option grants.

What did companies do? The right thing to do was to pick one or the other. A company could legitimately choose to make highly attractive in the money grants, so long it convinced its shareholders that such grants were necessary and desirable and also complied with all of the proper accounting and tax rules. Or it could choose to make at the money grants, and take full advantage of their accounting and tax advantages.

A word about the process of making stock option grants is in order here. Stock options grants usually require approval by a sub-committee of the Board of Directors. This usually happens in one of two ways—either the company convenes an actual meeting of the sub-committee at which they approve the grants, or the company circulates "uniform written consents" to each member of the sub-committee and solicits their approval of the options grants in writing. Either way, the process is time-consuming. But with the stock market frothing as it was in the late 1990s—those days of irrational exuberance—time was money. A day or two difference in the stock option grant date could have a tremendous impact on the value of the grants.

A company could focus on process—adhering to their ordinary processes for approving stock options regardless of the resulting grant date and strike price—or try to change their process to be more agile. Or a company could focus on timing, trying to capitalize on the ever-changing value of the stock options by manipulating their processes achieve a particular grant date. The trouble with the timing approach is it's nearly impossible to know *in advance* which day will be the most advantageous grant date. Nonetheless, companies tried to be more nimble, often delegating the authority to approve option grants to a single corporate officer—which, as we have seen—was a near-perfect opportunity for abuse.

In the face of all these competing interests and pressures, what happened? Far too many companies seem to have succumbed to the temptation to make in the money grants that appeared—for all corporate intents and purposes—to be at the money grants. How did they achieve this sleight of hand? Backdating—in all of its myriad forms. Putting false dates on corporate grant documents—as alleged in Brocade—was by far the simplest fraudulent scheme, but the variations seem to be limited only by the perpetrators' imaginations. In Comverse, for example, the company's top officers—the former CEO, CFO and General Counsel—are alleged to have routinely backdated stock option grants, giving themselves and other employees the benefit of 20-20 hindsight. According to the SEC's complaint, they went so far as to create a secret slush fund by making backdated options grants to fictitious employees, and later used those options to recruit and retain key personnel. To hide the backdating scheme, they also allegedly altered corporate records and lied to the company's auditors. Unfortunately, in the course of our investigations, we are finding that schemes like the one alleged in Comverse were not so unusual. Given the extremes that many company's top-level executives were willing to go to, backdating must have appeared to offer the best of both worlds—employees enjoyed the dazzling paper profits and stock ownership opportunities of in the money grants, while the corporation enjoyed all the advantages of at the money grants.

But stepping back for a moment—you have to ask yourself, what were they thinking? Falsified documents? Forgeries? Secret slush funds? Fictitious employees? Lying to the auditors? There's something very wrong here. The matters we are pursuing involve blatant and intentional conduct—not to mention the accounting and tax consequences to the corporation in eventually unwinding the scheme. And the scope of the unwinding consequences alone is enormous. The Associated Press reported last week that the companies that have publicly disclosed backdating problems to date will collectively incur costs of more than $10.3 billion in lost share price and additional compensation expenses.[1] The AP also reported 41 senior executives have left 20 companies involved in the backdating scandal,[2] and the total rises every week. Many companies have lost an entire generation of seasoned executives who have resigned or been fired as a result of the options scandal—undoubtedly causing enormous disruption and upheavals at the affected companies. Aside from the prospect of an SEC enforcement investigation and possible criminal liability, options backdating in all its various forms has left the companies involved in an accounting, tax and human resources quagmire. The good news is that the death knell on backdating has tolled because the motivation and opportunity to backdate has been substantially (though not entirely) eliminated due to a combination of new accounting rules that went into effect in 2005 requiring the expensing of all options, and the two-business-day reporting requirement for grants that became effective in 2002. Of course, we have been looking for more recent violations as well.

What lessons can we draw from all of this? I've given it some thought, and I think most of the lessons to be learned are consistent with what we all recognize as basic common sense.

*First,* beware the morphing monster—and its unintended consequences. Tools devised for one purpose can have dramatic unintended consequences when employed for different purposes in a different legal and tax environment. We've seen this happen over and over again. One example is the "Special Purpose Entity" or "SPE," which was designed as a special form of off-balance sheet accounting originally used in the aircraft industry. But SPEs migrated into other industries and morphed into a monster that was used extensively by the likes of Enron in perpetrating financial frauds. Another example is financial research—once a quiet backwater in financial services firms. When used as a tool by investment bankers, however, research reports morphed into a monster that clinched banking deals and drove IPO prices sky high—often regardless of the merits of the company, the true opinions of the analysts or the financial consequences to shareholders. Similarly, stock options were initially developed in the 1980s as an anti-takeover device, but because of unrelated changes in the tax and accounting rules, they morphed into a means of providing non-salary performance-based compensation, which was not their original purpose. And as we have seen, to the extent that stock option grants were viewed in the 1990s as a means of better aligning the interests of management and corporate shareholders by linking executive compensation to performance, they had yet another set of unintended consequences. Through backdating, stock options grants were used by some companies as a means of providing compensation that was entirely independent of performance. How did stock option grants become a monster? While most companies would ordinarily grant stock options through a specific and defined process that ensured legal compliance and fairness, many companies appear to have abandoned or compromised their processes in granting stock options. Once released from the restraints of process, stock option grants were allowed to run amok.

*Second,* your mother was right—just because your best friend jumps off a bridge doesn't mean you should too. Clearly, a lot of companies were involved in options backdating, but that doesn't excuse the fundamentally fraudulent nature of the scheme. If the only reason that can be offered as a justification for backdating is that "everyone else was doing it," that's a poor excuse for what amounts to unjust enrichment of a few employees at the expense of corporate shareholders.

*Third,* the simplest and most obvious lesson, you can't have your cake and eat it too. A stock option can be granted either in the money or at the money, but not both. You can take your pick, but you have to accept the consequences of your choice.

*Fourth,* process can be your friend. This is a variant of the "sunscreen and dental floss" rule. You see, both sunscreen and dental floss can have tremendous benefits, but only if you use them every single day. In the same way, if a company devises a specific lawful process for granting employee stock options and always follows it, there should be no problem explaining how, when and at what price any particular options were granted. The problems we are seeing with stock option abuses often seem to occur when a company abandons its regular process and starts to award stock options on an ad hoc basis. Like a hiker who strays off the path and into the wilderness, without the familiar signposts it's easy to get lost. If a particular grant process isn't working, then it should be changed. But the existence of a process and a company's adherence to it tends to ensure that the matter has been given careful consideration and is in the company's best interests. From a compliance perspective, creating and following a consistent process for awarding stock options seems to me to be something of a "no-brainer." Executive compensation is obviously an area where effective internal controls are critical. Like related party transactions, executive compensation is an important issue for boards of directors. Compared to other internal control measures, creating a standard process and a fixed schedule for the award of stock option compensation is relatively easy and inexpensive, especially when you consider the reported costs of backdating to companies involved. By following a standard options grant process, a company gets fair and transparent results, and there should be no random anomalies to explain. This brings me to another lesson.

The *fifth* lesson: If you are ever in doubt about whether any particular practice is right, imagine explaining it to your family, especially your children. This "explain-it-to-your-family" exercise has two advantages. To start with, you have to simplify and distill whatever it is you're contemplating down to its essence. The very process of simplifying the concept to its essence will usually enable you to see its true strengths and weaknesses. The other advantage is that you're pitching your plan to a supportive audience, but one that will give you their real opinions. If you want a really objective view of what you're doing, try asking a teenage boy. Teenage boys will tell you, in detail, all the flaws in your plan, and, for that matter, everything else you're doing. If you want more support, you might try your spouse—well, that depends. But if you can't imagine explaining to your children or other family members why what you're contemplating is the right thing to do, then you shouldn't do it. If you think about it, family members (except certain teenage boys) are the most sympathetic audience you're ever likely to face, so if you can't explain why it's right to them, it probably isn't right. In my prior career as a federal criminal prosecutor, whenever we won a guilty verdict from a jury, and fortunately we usually did, one of the hardest things was to watch the front row of the gallery—where the spouses and children sit—when a defendant stood up for sentencing.

*Finally,* what we have learned from stock options backdating—and from every other scandal in the financial markets in recent years—is that character matters. Corporate character matters—and employees take their cues from the top. In our experience, the character of the CEO and other top officers is generally reflected in the character of the entire company. If a CEO is known for his integrity, integrity becomes the corporate norm. If, on the other hand, a company's top executives are more interested in personal enrichment at the expense of the shareholders, our backdating investigations demonstrate yet again that other employees will follow suit.

In this regard, I am gratified to see that we have learned something from Enron and all that followed, particularly the enactment of the Sarbanes-Oxley Act, insofar as it has highlighted the critical importance of corporate governance. I spoke a few moments ago about the importance of process. Corporate governance is itself a process, which, when given due regard, ensures the integrity of the corporation and its conduct. I want to congratulate the Rock Center for all of the work it has done since its foundation earlier this year to address corporate governance issues, and to thank you all for your kind attention.

## End Notes

[1] Ellen Simon, Options Backdating: *Lost Share Price, Additional Compensation Total More Than $10 Billion, Assoc.* Press, Oct. 24, 2006.

[2] Id.

In: Backdating of Stock Options
Editor: Bernard T. Weinstein
ISBN: 978-1-60741-984-6


*Chapter 3*

# STOCK OPTIONS BACKDATING HEARING—COX TESTIMONY

*Christopher Cox*

Chairman Shelby, Ranking Member Sarbanes, and Members of the Committee:

Thank you for inviting me to testify today about options backdating. This issue is one of intense public interest because it strikes at the heart of the relationship among a public company's management, its directors, and its shareholders. I appreciate the opportunity to explain the Commission's initiatives to deal with abuses involving the backdating of options.

I am especially pleased to testify together with Chairman Mark Olson of the Public Company Accounting Oversight Board. I will let Chairman Olson speak to the steps the PCAOB is taking to address these issues from the auditing regulator's perspective, but I'd like to assure the Committee, and the public, that the Commission is working in close cooperation with the PCAOB in this important area.

There are many variations on the backdating theme. But here is a typical example of what some companies did: They granted an "in-the-money" option—that is, an option with an exercise price lower than that day's market price. They did this by misrepresenting the date of the option grant, to make it appear that the grant was made on an earlier date when the market value was lower. That, of course, is what is meant by abusive "backdating" in today's parlance.

The purpose of disguising an in-the-money option through backdating is to allow the person who gets the option grant to realize larger potential gains—without the company having to show it as compensation on the financial statements.

Rather obviously, this fact pattern results in a violation of the SEC's disclosure rules, a violation of accounting rules, and also a violation of the tax laws.

The SEC has been after the problem of abusive options backdating for several years. As a preliminary step in explaining the Commission's response to the problem of fraudulent options backdating, it would be useful to put the whole topic of options compensation into some perspective.

As you know, during the last year the Commission has been intensely focused on the quality of disclosure of executive compensation. Very recently, we enacted new rules that will require, beginning with the next proxy season, the full disclosure of all aspects of executive and director pay and benefits. A key component of that disclosure will be compensation in the form of stock options, which has been a fast growing portion of executive pay since the early 1990s.

Under the new SEC rules, all of an executive's compensation will now be totaled into one number, so that it can be compared easily from person to person, company to company, and industry to industry. The new rules also require detailed disclosure of compensation in the form of stock options, which will show whether a company has backdated options, and if so, why. The purpose of the new executive compensation rules is to make the CEO's pay understandable to the shareholders who own the company.

Of course, no new SEC rules would be necessary to make executive pay transparent, if executives were all paid in the form of salary. But beyond the obvious fact that the income tax code discriminates in favor of non-salary compensation that can be taxed as capital gains, one of the most significant reasons that non-salary forms of compensation have ballooned since the early 1990s is the $1 million legislative cap on salaries for certain top public company executives that was added to the Internal Revenue Code in 1993.

As a Member of Congress at the time, I well remember that the stated purpose was to control the rate of growth in CEO pay. With complete hindsight, we can now all agree that this purpose was not achieved. Indeed, this tax law change deserves pride of place in the Museum of Unintended Consequences.

There are other accounting and tax reasons, as well, that stock options over the years were increasingly included in the compensation packages of executives and non-executives.

Beginning in 1972, the accounting rule was that employee stock options wouldn't have to be shown as an expense on the income statement—so long as the terms were fixed when the option was granted, and so long as the exercise price was equal to the market price on that day. Indeed, no expense would ever need to be recorded in the financial statements for fixed options that weren't granted in-the-money.

In addition to this favorable accounting treatment, there was a tax benefit. The million-dollar cap on the tax deductibility of executive compensation, which I mentioned earlier, doesn't apply to options granted at fair market value. So for companies that wanted or needed to pay compensation in excess of $1 million per year, the tax code outlawed deducting it if it was paid in a straightforward way through salary, but permitted a deduction if the compensation was paid through at-the-money options.

And of course there were other reasons, many of them good ones with solid economic rationales, that companies wanted to use options as a form of compensation. For example, a properly-structured option plan can be useful in more closely aligning the incentives of shareholders and managers. And for growth companies, the use of stock options as compensation offers a way to conserve resources while attracting top-flight talent in highly competitive markets.

All of these factors have contributed to the now-widespread use of stock options as compensation. But just as option compensation increased, so did the potential for abuse. And Congress deserves credit for taking preemptive action that we now know was critical to stopping the spread of the backdating contagion.

Four years ago, in 2002, the Sarbanes-Oxley Act very presciently tightened up on the reporting of stock option grants. Before Sarbanes-Oxley, officers and directors didn't have to disclose their receipt of stock option grants until after the end of the fiscal year in which the transaction took place. So a grant in January might not have to be disclosed until more than a year later. SOX changed that, by requiring real-time disclosure of option grants. And in August 2002, shortly after the law was signed, the SEC issued rules requiring that officers and directors disclose any option grants within two business days.

Not only must option grants now be reported within two business days, but this information was among the first required to be filed electronically using interactive data. Thanks to this new data-tagging technology, the public now has almost instant access to information about stock option grants.

The following year, in 2003, the SEC took another important step that has helped increase the transparency of public company options plans. The Commission approved changes to the listing standards of the New York Stock Exchange and the Nasdaq Stock Market that for the first time required shareholder approval of almost all equity compensation plans. Companies have to publicly disclose the material terms of their stock option plans in order to obtain shareholder approval.

Very importantly, the required disclosures include the terms on which options will be granted. And companies must tell their shareholders whether the plan permits options to be granted with an exercise price that's less than the market value on the date of grant.

Then, in December 2004, the FASB issued Statement of Financial Accounting Standard 123R, which effectively eliminated the accounting advantage that had previously been given to stock options issued at-the-money. Since this new accounting rule took effect, all stock options granted to employees have to be recorded as an expense in the financial statements, whether or not the exercise price is at fair market value. This rule is nearly fully phased in.

Most recently, in January of this year, the SEC proposed that public companies be required to more thoroughly disclose their awards of in-the-money options to certain executives. The Commission also proposed that companies be required to disclose the fair value of the option on the grant date, as determined under the new accounting rules. The Commission adopted final rules on these subjects on July 26, 2006. As a result, in the next proxy season beginning in the spring, all public companies will now report this information in clear, easy to understand tabular presentations.

The tables will include:

- The grant date fair value under FAS 123R (which is aggregated in the total compensation amount that is shown for each named executive officer);
- The FAS 123R grant date;
- The closing market price on the grant date if it is greater than the exercise price of the option; and
- The date the compensation committee or full board of directors took action to grant the option, if that date is different than the grant date.

Because the dates and numbers often don't tell the whole story, companies will also be required to discuss the policies and goals of their compensation programs—in plain English. The reports to investors will describe whether, and if so how, a company has engaged (or might engage in the future) in backdating or any of the many variations on that theme concerning the timing and pricing of options. For example, if a company has a plan to issue option grants in coordination with the release of material non-public information, that will now be clearly described.

The Commission will continue to avail itself of every opportunity to clarify the rules and procedures for options issuance going forward. To that end, you can expect that the Office of the Chief Accountant will soon issue further public guidance on the accounting issues surrounding backdating.

So, to recap, here is what has been done by way of prophylactic rules to eliminate the opportunities for abusive backdating. First, Sarbanes-Oxley has closed the disclosure loophole that permitted months and sometimes more than a year to elapse before option grants had to be reported. Second, a new accounting rule—FAS 123R—has eliminated the accounting benefit of granting at-the-money options. And third, the SEC's brand new executive compensation rules now require a complete quantitative and narrative disclosure of a company's executive compensation plans and goals. That enhanced disclosure will make it clear whenever options are being backdated, and it will require an explanation of the reasons. These new rules will soon be complemented by additional accounting guidance on these subjects.

Each of these steps by itself is an important contribution to preventing backdating abuse. In combination, they have effectively slammed the door shut on the easy opportunities to get away with secretive options grants. That's why almost all of the stock option abuses our Enforcement Division has uncovered started in periods prior to these reforms.

But while these accounting and disclosure rules changes have made it easier to detect and punish backdating abuses going forward, uncovering the problems from prior years has been quite a challenge.

A few years ago, the SEC began working with academics to decipher market data that provided the first clues something fishy was going on. One of the academics with whom the SEC worked was Erik Lie of the University of Iowa, who subsequently published a paper in 2005 that showed compelling circumstantial evidence of backdating.

Dr. Lie's data showed that before 2003, a surprising number of companies seemed to have had an uncanny ability to choose grant dates that coincided with low stock prices. (In a follow-up paper this year, co-authored with Dr.

Randall Heron of Indiana University, Dr. Lie demonstrated that this problem has greatly diminished since 2002, when the Sarbanes-Oxley Act shortened the time for reporting option grants to two business days.)

With a fair amount of detective work, and with the aid of economic research conducted by the SEC's Office of Economic Analysis, the Commission succeeded in turning what had begun as mere evidentiary threads into solid leads. Eventually, some of the evidence we began turning up was so compelling that several U.S. Attorneys took a criminal interest. Over the past several years, our inventory of backdating and related investigations has grown substantially. And beginning three years ago, the SEC has brought several enforcement actions against companies and individuals for fraudulent option practices.

For example, in 2003, the Commission charged Peregrine Systems, Inc. with financial fraud for failing to record any expense for compensation when it issued incentive stock options. The SEC's complaint alleged that at each quarterly board meeting, the company's directors would approve a total number of options for employees. The company would then allocate the options to the employees during the quarter. But the options wouldn't be priced until the day after the next quarterly Board meeting. On that day, the company looked back at the market price of its stock between the two quarterly Board meetings, and picked the lowest price. That turned the options into in-the-money grants. But even though accounting rules required that they then be recorded as compensation expense, the company didn't do that. As a result, Peregrine understated its expenses by approximately $90 million.

The following year, in 2004, the SEC brought a case involving the manipulation not of option grants, but of exercise dates. Our complaint charged that Symbol Technologies, Inc. and its former general counsel fudged option exercise dates so that senior executives could profit unfairly at the company's expense. Rather than use the actual exercise date as defined by the company's option plans, the general counsel picked the most advantageous date from a 30-day "look-back" period in order to come up with a lower exercise price. This was done without board approval or public disclosure. The SEC charged that to create the false appearance that these exercises had actually occurred on the chosen dates, the company's general counsel had instructed his staff to backdate the relevant documents, and to substitute phony exercise dates on the forms the executives used to report their option exercises to the SEC and the public. The result, according to the complaint, was a serious misstatement of the company's stock option expenses.

When the company subsequently restated its improper accounting, the cumulative net increase in reported stock option expenses was $229 million. The amount would undoubtedly have been higher had it not been for the passage of the Sarbanes-Oxley Act. Thanks to the Act's new two-day deadline for reporting options transactions by officers and its prohibition on company loans to officers and directors, the company and its general counsel had put a halt to the "look-backs" because the law had rendered the practice unfeasible.

While the alleged manipulations of option grants and exercises in these two cases were part of larger accounting fraud charges, two more recent cases have focused solely on option practices. These are the Brocade and Comverse actions that the SEC filed in July and August of this year. The executives charged in these cases are contesting the SEC's allegations.

In July, the SEC filed a civil fraud action against three former executives of Brocade Communications Systems, alleging that the former CEO and the former Vice President of Human Resources routinely backdated stock option grants to give employees favorably priced options without recording the necessary compensation expenses. Specifically, the SEC's complaint alleges that the CEO caused Brocade to grant in-the-money options to both new and current employees between 2000 and 2004, and then backdated documents to make it appear that the options were at-the-money when granted. This had the effect of concealing millions of dollars in expenses from investors.

The complaint alleges that the CEO repeatedly used hindsight to select a date with a lower stock price from the recent past as the purported option grant date, and that, to facilitate the scheme, the Human Resources executive created, or directed others to create, false paperwork making it appear that the options had been granted on the earlier date. The complaint alleged that, in some instances, employment offer letters and compensation committee minutes were falsified to suggest that options had been granted to employees before they had even been hired by the company.

The SEC's complaint also charged Brocade's former CFO, alleging that he learned of the backdating after joining the company but took no action to correct or halt the practice and instead signed Brocade's SEC filings. When these stock option practices surfaced, Brocade was required to restate and revise its financial statements for six fiscal years, from 1999 through 2004. The scheme resulted in the inflation of Brocade's net income by as much as $1 billion in the year 2000 alone. Simultaneously with the filing of the SEC's complaint, the U.S. Attorney's Office for the Northern District of California separately filed criminal charges against the former CEO and the former Vice President of Human Resources for the same misconduct.

In the second recent case, the Commission filed a civil fraud complaint last month against three former senior executives of Comverse Technology, Inc., alleging that they engaged in a decade-long fraudulent scheme to grant undisclosed, in-the-money options to themselves and to others by backdating stock option grants to coincide with historically low closing prices of Comverse common stock.

The complaint alleges that from 1991 to 2002, Comverse's founder and former Chairman and CEO repeatedly used hindsight to select a date when the closing price of Comverse's common stock was at or near a quarterly or annual low. According to the complaint, the CEO then communicated this date and closing price to Comverse's former general counsel who, with the CEO's knowledge, created company records that falsely indicated that a committee of Comverse's board of directors had actually approved the option grant on the date the CEO had picked.

The complaint also alleges that Comverse's former CFO joined the scheme no later than 1998, and assisted in selecting backdated grant dates. It is alleged that each of the three defendants realized actual illicit gains from the backdating when they sold stock they acquired from exercises of backdated options, including at least $6 million by the CEO alone. In addition, the complaint alleges that the former CEO and CFO created a slush fund of backdated options between 1999 and 2002 by causing options to be granted to fictitious employees and, later, used these options to recruit and retain key personnel.

Comverse has publicly announced that it expects to restate historical financial results for multiple years in order to record material charges for option-related compensation expenses. Simultaneously with the filing of the SEC's complaint, the U.S Attorney's Office for the Eastern District of New York unsealed a criminal complaint charging these three executives with conspiracy to violate the antifraud provisions of the federal securities laws, wire fraud, and mail fraud by engaging in the same scheme.

These cases demonstrate some of the variations on the basic theme of fraudulent backdating that the Commission has uncovered. They involve backdated option grants that are more profitable to recipients; backdated option exercises that reduce recipients' taxes at the expense of shareholders; options granted to top executives; and options granted to rank and file employees. They involve actual personal gain to wrongdoers, and real harm to companies that failed to properly account for the options practices.

Unfortunately, these cases that I've used as illustrations are not the only matters the SEC has under investigation. The SEC's Division of Enforcement is currently investigating over 100 companies concerning possible fraudulent reporting of stock option grants. The companies are located throughout the country, and include Fortune 500 companies as well as smaller cap issuers. They span multiple industry sectors.

You should not expect that all of these investigations will result in enforcement proceedings. At the same time, we have to expect other enforcement actions will be forthcoming in the future.

The SEC's Enforcement staff is sharing information related to its investigations with other law enforcement and regulatory authorities as warranted and appropriate, including the Department of Justice, the President's Corporate Fraud Task Force, U.S. Attorney's offices around the country, the Federal Bureau of Investigation, and the Internal Revenue Service.

In our rulemaking, our provision of accounting and final regulatory guidance, and our enforcement programs, the SEC has been and will remain vigilant in the battle against fraudulent options backdating. The agency is grateful for the opportunity to provide you with this update on a very important subject. I am happy to take any questions you may have.

In: Backdating of Stock Options
Editor: Bernard T. Weinstein
ISBN: 978-1-60741-984-6


*Chapter 4*

# STOCK OPTIONS BACKDATING HEARING— LIE TESTIMONY

***Erik Lie***

Chairman Shelby, Ranking Member Sarbanes and Members of the Committee:

Thank you for inviting me to testify today about stock options backdating. In theory, stock options can be used to motivate executives and other employees to create value for shareholders. However, they have also been used to (i) conceal true compensation expenses, (ii) cheat on corporate taxes, and (iii) siphon money away from shareholders to option recipients. I will take this opportunity to offer some background on stock options and stock option grants, describe the practice of backdating, and make some recommendations for the future.

## BACKGROUND ON STOCK OPTIONS AND STOCK OPTION GRANTS

Let me first provide some background on and mention some key aspects of executive stock options and option grants.

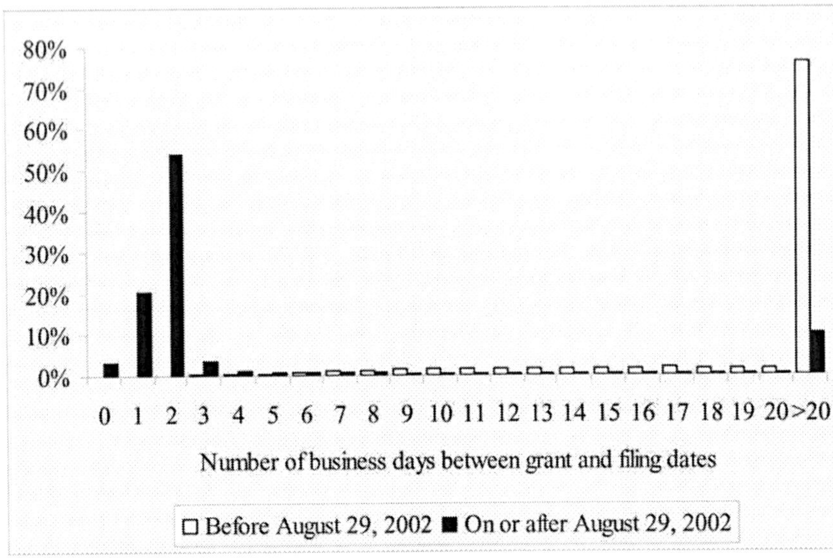


- A stock option gives its owner the right to buy the stock of the company in the future.
- Stock options are granted to executives at various intervals. It is common to grant options once a year, though it is also possible for executives not to be granted options in a year or to be granted options numerous times in a year. In most cases, there is no fixed schedule to these grants, meaning that they do not occur on the same date (e.g., on July 1) in consecutive years.
- Before August 29, 2002, executive option grants had to be filed anywhere from 10 business days to more than a year after the grant, depending on (i) when a grant occurred within a calendar month and fiscal year and (ii) whether a Form 4 or Form 5 was used when filing the grants with the SEC. Under the current regulations that took effect on August 29, 2002 as part of the Sarbanes-Oxley Act, option grants to executives have to be filed with the Securities and Exchange Commission (SEC) within two business days. Distributions of the number of days between the official grant date and the filing date based on a sample of about 40,000 grants to top executives between 1996 and 2005 are given in the graph below. The new filing requirement dramatically reduced the lag between the grant date and the filing date. Importantly, about 22% of grants since August 29,

2002 were filed late, and almost 10% were filed at least one month late.

- Most options granted to executives expire after exactly 10 years.
- The price at which the stock can be bought is determined at the time of the grant and generally does not change. It is called the "exercise price" or the "strike price."
- Most executive stock options are granted "at-the-money," i.e., the exercise price is set to equal the stock price on the day of the grant. ("In-the-money" means that the exercise price is below the stock price, and "out-of-the-money" means that the exercise price is above the stock price.)
- In a sample of 40,000 grants from 1996 to 2005, the exercise price matches the closing price on the grant day in 50% of the cases and the closing price on the day before the grant day in 12% of the cases.
- There are several reasons why options are granted at-the-money:
  - Accounting Principles Board (APB) Opinion No. 25, which was phased out in 2005, allowed companies to expense options according to the intrinsic value method, whereby the expense equals the difference between the fair value of the underlying stock and the exercise price of the option. Under this rule, at-the-money options did not have to be charged against reported earnings. (Under FAS 123R, which replaced APB 25, companies have to expense the fair market value of the options at the time of the grant.)
  - Unlike in-the-money grants, at-the-money grants qualify as performance-based compensation. As such, at-the-money grants receive favorable tax treatment under Section 162(m) of the Internal Revenue Code, which limits the deductibility of nonperformance-based compensation for tax purposes to one million dollars per executive.
  - Incentive stock options (ISOs), which are often a part of broad-based option plans that could qualify for more favorable tax treatment than non-qualified options at the individual level, cannot be granted in-the-money. Note, however, that most options granted to executives are non-qualified options (NQOs), and not ISOs, as ISOs are limited to a value of $100,000 per employee per calendar year and also count as income in the determination of the Alternative Minimum Tax (AMT).

- At-the-money grants might be perceived as a better incentive mechanism than in-the-money options, because executives are only rewarded if the stock price increases.
- The practice of granting options at-the-money provides the incentives to time the grant to occur on a day when the stock price was particularly low and/or to manipulate the information flow around the grant date. (Note that these incentives would be present for in-the-money and out-of-the money grants also, provided that the exercise price is a function of the stock price, e.g., 90% or 110% of the stock price.)
- Some potential strategies that might be used to inflate the value of option grants include the following:
    - *Spring-loading/Bullet-dodging:* The terms "spring-loading" and "bullet-dodging" refer to the practices of timing option grants to take place before expected good news or after expected bad news, respectively. They have also been referred to as "forward dating."

    - *Manipulation of the information flow:* This refers to the practice of timing corporate announcements relative to known future option grant dates. For example, if a firm will soon announce a share repurchase plan that is expected to raise the stock price, this announcement might be postponed until after the option grant.

    - *Backdating:* This refers to the practice of cherry-picking a date from the past when the stock price was relatively low to be the official grant date.

## RESEARCH ON OPTION GRANT TIMING

In a 1997 study entitled "Good timing: CEO stock option awards and company news announcements," David Yermack of New York University reported that the average abnormal stock return during the months after option grants to CEOs between 1992 and 1994 exceeds 2%, which he interpreted as evidence that the grants are timed to occur before anticipated stock price increases (i.e., spring-loading).

In a 2000 study entitled "CEO stock option awards and the timing of corporate voluntary disclosures," David Aboody of UCLA and Ron Kasznik of Stanford University reported that the average abnormal stock return is positive even for a subsample of grants between 1992 and 1996 that appear to be scheduled. They interpreted this as evidence that the information flow around grants is manipulated.

In my 2005 study entitled "On the timing of CEO stock option awards," I documented negative abnormal stock returns before and positive returns after CEO option grants between 1992 and 2002, and these trends intensified over time. I further reported that the portion of the stock returns that is predicted by overall market factors exhibits a similar pattern, prompting my conclusion that "unless executives have an informational advantage that allows them to develop superior forecasts regarding the future market movements that drive these predicted returns, the results suggest that the official grant date must have been set retroactively" (p. 811).

In a soon-to-be-published study entitled "Does backdating explain the stock price pattern around executive stock option grants?" that I coauthored with Randy Heron of Indiana University, we found further evidence in support of my earlier backdating argument. As noted earlier, a provision in Sarbanes-Oxley reduces the SEC filing requirement for new option grants to two days from the earlier requirements that allowed executives to report grants up to several months after the grant date. To the extent that companies comply with this new requirement, backdating should be greatly curbed. Thus, if backdating explains the stock price pattern around option grants, the price pattern should diminish following the new requirements. Indeed, we found that the stock price pattern is much weaker since the new reporting requirements took effect. Any remaining pattern is concentrated on the couple of days between the reported grant date and the filing date (when backdating still might work), and for longer periods for the minority of grants that violate the two-day reporting requirements. I replicated these results in the figure below using a sample of about 40,000 grants to top executives during the period 1996-2005. We interpreted the findings as strong evidence that backdating explains most of the abnormal price pattern around option grants.

In an unpublished study entitled "What fraction of stock option grants to top executives have been backdated or manipulated?" Randy Heron and I used a sample of 39,888 grants to top executives across 7,774 companies between 1996 and 2005 to estimate the following:

- 14% of all grants to top executives dated between 1996 and 2005 were backdated or otherwise manipulated.

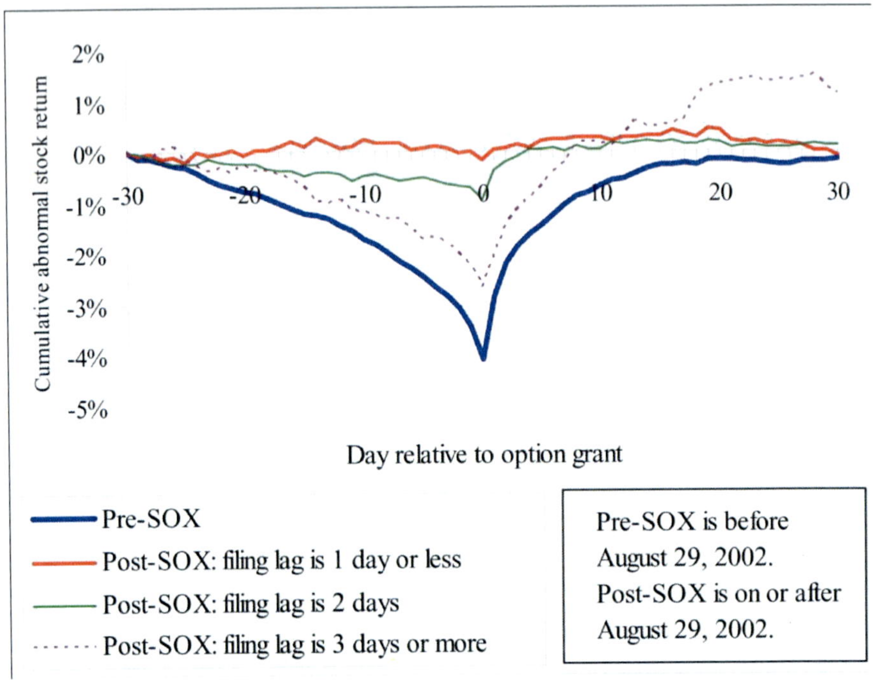


- 23% of unscheduled, at-the-money grants to top executives dated between 1996 and August 2002 were backdated or otherwise manipulated.
- This fraction was more than halved to 10% as a result of the new two-day reporting requirement that took effect in August 2002.
  - Among the minority of unscheduled, at-the-money grants after August 2002 that were filed late (i.e., more than two business days after the purported grant dates), 20% were backdated or otherwise manipulated.
  - Among the majority of unscheduled, at-the-money grants after August 2002 that were filed on time, 7% were backdated or otherwise manipulated. (The benefit of backdating is naturally greatly reduced in such cases.)
- The prevalence of backdating differs across firm characteristics; backdating is more common among
  - tech firms,
  - small and medium firms (i.e., those with a market capitalization less than $1 billion), and
  - firms with high stock price volatility .

- The auditing firm is only modestly associated with the incidence of backdating.
    - PricewaterhouseCoopers is associated with a slightly lower fraction of backdated grants after controlling for other factors.
    - Non-big-five auditing firms are associated with a higher fraction of both late filings and unscheduled grants, which appear to result in more backdating.
- 29% of firms that granted options to top executives between 1996 and 2005 manipulated one or more of these grants in some fashion.

## IS OPTION GRANT TIMING ILLEGAL?

There is an ongoing debate regarding whether spring-loading and bullet-dodging are illegal. These practices have been compared to insider trading of stock. The debate hinges on the definition of the "harmed party." In regular insider trading cases, one party in the transaction possesses inside information that the other party (the harmed party) does not possess. In cases of option grants, some have argued that both parties, i.e., the option recipient and the Board of Directors of the firm that grants the options, have access to the same inside information, so it is not the case that the option recipient exploits an informational advantage. The other point of view is that insiders, with the consent of the Board of Directors, are using their informational advantage to extract additional compensation from the firm's owners (shareholders). Under this viewpoint, the harmed party would be the firm's existing shareholders, who do not possess the same information, and whose ownership value is reduced to a greater degree than would otherwise be the case.

Backdating is less ambiguous. If options purported to be at-the-money on the backdated grant date were in-the-money on the actual grant date (which should be the measurement date for financial and tax reporting purposes) and not properly accounted for, then

- the firm's reported earnings were too high according to the accounting regulations (under both APB 25 and FAS 123R),
- the firm's taxes might have been too low (due to IRC § 162(m), and because the deductible spread between the exercise price and the stock price at the time of the actual option exercises is artificially inflated),

- if the options are ISOs, one of their requirements for their favored tax-status have been violated, and
- any requirement in the option plan that the options should be granted at the fair market value is violated.
- In addition, to implement the backdating strategy, documents might have been forged, which is a federal offense.

## CONCLUSION

Backdating of option grants was a pervasive practice among publicly traded corporations in the U.S. in the late 1990s and the beginning of this century. My own research suggests that spring-loading, bullet-dodging, and manipulation of the information flow was either significantly less prevalent or less successful in the aggregate in producing immediate gains for the option recipients during the same period.

The problem of backdating can be eliminated by requiring grants to be filed electronically with the SEC on the same day that they are granted. Given that (i) the form for filing this information is very simple and (ii) the forms can be filed online, this is a reasonable requirement, and, in fact, some grants are already filed on the grant date. Of course, this requirement has to be strictly enforced with appropriate penalties for any violation, such that the frequency of late filing that is evident for the last few years is greatly reduced.

As the problem of backdating is eliminated, the problems of spring-loading, bullet-dodging and manipulation of the information flow might become more prominent. Thus, it is critical to clarify whether these alternative strategies are legal. If so, restrictions to minimize their occurrence should be developed. In particular, options should not be granted near major corporate announcements. Further, there should be timely and complete disclosure of grants.

Finally, to eliminate timing relative to recent stock prices, the benchmark stock price should be the price on the grant date. For example, if the options are granted at-the-money, the exercise price should be set to equal the stock price on the grant day rather than the stock price on the prior day, which is a fairly common practice (see earlier statistics). This eliminates the possibility that options are granted on a day when the price has increased significantly but the prior day's lower price is used for contracting purposes.

In: Backdating of Stock Options
Editor: Bernard T. Weinstein
ISBN: 978-1-60741-984-6


*Chapter 5*

# STOCK OPTIONS BACKDATING HEARING— OLSON TESTIMONY

*Mark W. Olson*

Chairman Shelby, Ranking Member Sarbanes, and Members of the Committee:

I am pleased to appear today on behalf of the Public Company Accounting Oversight Board to discuss the PCAOB's response to concerns relating to certain stock option granting practices.

The PCAOB oversees the auditors of public companies, in order to protect the interests of the investing public in the preparation of informative, accurate and independent audit reports on public company financial statements. The PCAOB does not regulate accounting or disclosures by public companies; rather, the PCAOB's role is to enhance the quality of the audits of such financial statements. Simply put, the PCAOB's job is to improve the quality and reliability of public company audits, so that investors can have more confidence in audited financial statements.

The Board has a variety of tools with which to promote improved audit quality. While those tools include meaningful enforcement and disciplinary authority – important authority backing up all of our other authority – the Board has focused on implementing a supervisory model of regulation intended to focus firms on the need for high quality auditing, by helping them see where they are falling short and providing feedback and guidance that facilitates their efforts to improve. The PCAOB's approach to the audit issues that arise in connection with companies' stock option granting practices is an example of the PCAOB's emphasis on real-time improvements in audit quality.

# I. Stock Option Granting Practices Have Raised Concerns about Companies' Accounting for and Disclosure of Compensation Costs

Before describing the PCAOB's response to concerns about some companies stock option granting practices, I will briefly describe the history of these concerns and certain regulatory changes that appear to have reduced the opportunity and incentive for some of the practices at issue.

## A. Employee Stock Options Can Be a Useful Tool, but Concerns Have Arisen Whether Companies Have Properly Disclosed Their True Costs

As we all know, many companies issue stock options as a form of compensation and to give employees vested interests in improving their companies' performance and share prices. Such options usually give employees the right to buy shares in the future, at the price of the stock on the date of the grant. The higher the share price rises relative to the exercise price, the more valuable the options are. Well managed, stock options can be a useful and appropriate tool to attract and retain employees.

Companies' financial statements, of course, must account for and disclose options consistent with applicable accounting and regulatory requirements, and recently concerns have arisen that some may not have done so. More than 120 companies have announced they are involved in civil or criminal investigations, or internal reviews, of possible problems in the way they have granted, accounted for and disclosed stock option compensation to senior executives and other employees. Academic studies have long noted suspiciously favorable patterns related to the timing of option grants. Those patterns were largely attributed to companies planning option grants in advance of significant releases of information, until a 2005 study by University of Iowa researcher's Erik Lie, who I understand will discuss his work in the second panel of this hearing.[1] That study suggested that the favorable granting patterns could be attributable to companies having retroactively assigned option grant dates on dates their stocks hit relative lows, when the options were in fact granted weeks or months later.

## B. Changes in Regulatory Requirements Appear to Have Reduced the Incidence of Suspiciously-timed Option Grants

While the extent of the problems arising from backdating and other stock option granting practices is not yet clear, two significant changes in the disclosure and accounting for stock option grants in recent years – the first initiated by, and the second supported by, this Committee – seem to have significantly reduced companies' opportunity and incentive to backdate grants.

First, the Sarbanes-Oxley Act appears to have significantly reduced the incidence of backdated option grants. Specifically, the SEC's rules implementing Section 403 of the Act now require public company officers and directors to report their receipt of stock options within two days of the grant.[2] Previously, such persons were generally not required to report option grants until 45 days after the fiscal year in which they were received.[3] Given the new filing requirement, the ability to backdate option grants to coincide with low stock prices is greatly curtailed. Indeed, subsequent research has shown that, following the change, when company insiders reported options within the new deadline, there was little to no pattern of abnormal share price increases soon afterward.[4]

Second, accounting standards for employee stock options have also gone through several changes over the last few years. Historically, the applicable accounting standard – found in Accounting Principles Board Opinion No. 25 – required companies to record, as compensation cost, the amount, if any, by which the price of an employee stock option exceeded the market price on the date of the grant.[5] Compensation expenses associated with such "in-the-money" stock options was required to be reported as incurred in the period or periods in which the employee performed services for the option, which could extend for years after the option grant.[6] As a result, failure to account properly for in-the-money options could affect several financial periods.

APB Opinion No. 25 permitted companies not to record any cost, however, when employee stock options were granted at a price equal to or greater than the market price on the date of the grant. APB Opinion No. 25 thus discouraged companies from granting options at less than the prevailing market price, although such discounted options could be more lucrative for recipients. Some companies may have attempted to have it both ways, though, by granting options at prices below market on the date of the grant but treating them for accounting and tax purposes as if they were granted on a date when market prices were lower.

In 1994, the Financial Accounting Standards Board adopted Statement of Financial Accounting Standards No. 123, which encouraged companies to report the cost of stock option grants to employees at their fair value, but permitted them to continue to rely on APB Opinion No. 25, so long as they disclosed what the compensation cost would have been had they recorded such options at their fair value.[7] Finally, in 2004, the FASB eliminated APB Opinion No. 25 and, beginning with financial statements for annual periods starting after June 15, 2005, required companies to account for employee stock options at their fair value, regardless of any difference between an option's exercise price and the market price at the time of grant.[8]

## II. The PCAOB Has Alerted Auditors to Use Judgment in Considering Issues Relating to Stock Option Granting Practices in Their Audits

Although much of the conduct currently under review appears to predate the Sarbanes-Oxley Act, errors related to such conduct may affect current period financial statements if employee performance related to past option grants continues into the present. That is, if an employee is still earning an option through performance (e.g., the option has not vested yet) then any compensation cost associated with the option may be allocable to the current financial period. In addition, new revelations of such conduct may trigger current auditor obligations with respect to past financial periods.

As the prevalence of problems in dating of stock option grants became clear, the PCAOB considered the implications of such problems for audits, and developed a strategy to draw those issues to auditors' attention so that they can address them in this year's audits. Specifically, the PCAOB reviewed patterns in option granting practices identified in available research, accounting firms' existing guidance to their auditors related to option granting practices, and auditing, accounting and regulatory requirements that have a bearing on audits of stock option grants. In addition, the Board discussed issues related to the timing of stock option grants at the June 2006 public meeting of its Standing

Advisory Group.[9] With the encouragement of members of this advisory group, these efforts led to an Audit Practice Alert publicly issued by the Board's staff on July 28, and disseminated electronically to the more than 1,600 public accounting firms registered with the PCAOB. This tool allowed the PCAOB to provide real-time guidance as auditors begin a new audit season, without adding to the volume or complexity of the body of existing standards.

I have attached a copy of this Alert as Exhibit A. The Alert focuses auditors on several considerations related to evaluating and addressing in their audits the risk that stock option granting practices may have led to material misstatement of financial statements. In doing so, the Alert identifies existing standards that could bear on their work and applies them to the issues that have been raised regarding companies' stock option granting practices; the Alert does not establish new requirements.

Specifically, the Alert tells auditors that, in audits currently underway or to be performed in the future, they should use certain information that existing standards direct them to acquire, in order to assess the nature and potential magnitude of risks associated with their audit clients' stock option granting practices. The Alert also emphasizes that auditors must use professional judgment in making this assessment and in determining appropriate procedures to address any identified risks. In addition, the Alert reminds auditors of several procedural considerations, such as how they should approach requests for consents to use past audit opinions, including situations in which they are no longer the auditor of record. The Alert also describes circumstances in which existing standards require auditors to reconsider past audit opinions.

As the Alert points out, in assessing the risk of material misstatement of financial statements, an auditor should consider whether the company accounted for options that are still outstanding under APB Opinion No. 25. If so, and if a company granted options at a price that was lower than the market price on the true grant date, then the auditor should consider whether compensation costs were materially understated (and whether additional disclosures should have been made) in the periods of the recipientemployee's performance, including the current period. The Alert also instructs the auditor to consider the effect of any errors in measuring compensation on the effectiveness of the company's internal control over financial reporting. Finally, the Alert reminds auditors that errors in reported option compensation may have material tax implications for companies[10] and may result in material contingent obligations, including those due to pending legal and regulatory matters.

In closing, the Board appreciates the opportunity to describe how it has approached concerns about companies' accounting for employee stock options. Alerting auditors to practices and trends that may be relevant to their ongoing audits is a critical part of the PCAOB's approach to oversight. The Board's goal is to help auditors identify and address problems in financial reporting in order to protect investors' interests in high-quality and reliable audits. The PCAOB's work in the area of auditing employee stock option grants is an important step toward this goal.

I would be pleased to answer any questions.

## End Notes

[1] *See* Lie, E., "On the Timing of CEO Stock Option Awards," *Management Science* (May 2005), at 802, available at http://www.biz.uiowa.edu/faculty/elie/Grants-MS.pdf.

[2] *See* SEC Release No. 34-46421, Ownership Reports and Trading by Officers, Directors and Principal Security Holders (August 27, 2002), available at http://www.sec.gov/rules/final/34- 46421.htm. Section 403 of the Sarbanes-Oxley Act required certain company insiders to file reports of certain transactions in the securities of their companies within two days of the transaction. In addition, it required such reports to be filed electronically and available on a public, SEC Web site as well as on the company's Web site if it maintains one.

[3] Under Section 16 of the Securities Exchange Act of 1934, and the SEC's implementing rules, directors, officers and certain others are required to report transactions and holdings involving their companies' securities, including the receipt of employee stock options. Until August 29, 2002, stock options awarded under most employee stock purchase and other benefit plans were required to be reported (on the SEC's Form 5) within 45 days after the end of the fiscal year in which they were granted. In its rule implementing Section 403 of the Sarbanes-Oxley Act, the SEC required certain transactions that were formerly reportable annually on Form 5, such as option grants, to be reported, like other insider transactions, on Form 4 within Section 403's new two-day deadline.

[4] That research also shows that the previously identified pattern of stock prices rising shortly after grant dates has continued for those companies whose insiders have not complied with the two-day requirement. *See* Heron, R. and Lie, E., "Does Backdating Explain the Stock Price Pattern Around Executive Stock Option Grants?" forthcoming in *Journal of Financial Economics*, available at http://www.biz.uiowa.edu/faculty/elie/Grants-JFE.pdf.

[5] *See* Accounting Principles Board Opinion No. 25. Accounting Principles Board Opinions were promulgated by the American Institute of Certified Public Accountants until 1973, when the Financial Accounting Standards Board was established. At that time, the FASB adopted outstanding APB Opinions, as amended, and over time has superseded them.

[6] APB Opinion No. 25, para. 12.

[7] *See* Statement of Financial Accounting Standards No. 123, *Share-Based Payment*, available at http://www.fasb.org/pdf/fas123.pdf.

[8] *See* Statement of Financial Accounting Standards No. 123 (revised 2004), Share-Based Payments, available at http://www.fasb.org/pdf/fas123r.pdf; *see also* SEC Release No. 33-8568 (April 15, 2005). Certain small business issuers have until annual periods starting after December 15, 2005 to comply with FAS 123(R). Id.

[9] The Board convened its Standing Advisory Group pursuant to Section 103(a)(4) of the Sarbanes-Oxley Act. The Group consists of a select group of experts in auditing and financial reporting, including representatives of investors, accountants, and public companies and meets three times a year to advise the Board on its standards-setting responsibilities.

[10] The Internal Revenue Code limits the deduction public companies may take for compensation paid to certain executive officers to $1 million, but it excludes from this limit compensation that is performance-based. *See* Internal Revenue Code Section 162(m). Stock option compensation may be treated as performance-based when the exercise price is equal to or more than the grant date's market price. If, on the other hand, the option provides for a discounted exercise price, it counts toward, and is subject to tax if it exceeds, the deduction limit. Companies that may have granted stock options at an exercise price that differs from the market price on the grant date, may have a tax liability, and potentially penalties, for past taxes due. If material, auditors should confirm that these items are recorded and reported in the financial statements.

In: Backdating of Stock Options
Editor: Bernard T. Weinstein
ISBN: 978-1-60741-984-6


*Chapter 6*

# STOCK OPTIONS BACKDATING HEARING—READ TESTIMONY

***Russell Read***

Chairman Shelby, Senator Sarbanes and members of the Senate Banking Committee, I am pleased to be here today to provide an institutional investor's perspective on the important topic of stock option backdating and spring loading.

I am Russell Read, Chief Investment Officer with the California Public Employees' Retirement System (CalPERS). As you know, CalPERS is the nation's largest public pension system with more than $209 billion in assets. We have long been a voice for corporate governance. We are committed to executive compensation reform, to full disclosure and transparency of financial information, and to director accountability.

The recent allegations around secret and even fraudulent backdating of options are disturbing. We appreciate your leadership, Mr. Chairman in calling for this hearing and for your personal commitment and the commitment of the Senate Banking Committee toward addressing this problem.

CalPERS believes that as part of a good executive compensation policy, stock options are appropriate. They align employees' interest with that of the shareowners. But when options are hidden from view, and when the option awards themselves do not tie to performance, it creates a serious problem.

As you know, CalPERS size does not lend itself to selling our stocks in troubled companies. As a large institutional investor, we don't have the luxury of not showing up for the ballgame. Baseball fans can choose to stay home, but as the steward for so many public servants who depend on us for their retirement security, we cannot.

If we are out of the ball game, we can't produce the investment returns that cover $3 of every $4 of our people's retirement benefits.

When an executive takes stealth payments that we can't trace, when companies make false statements and omit material facts concerning backdating of option grant, billions of dollars can be inappropriately given and once the truth of such option grant practices are made, it can cause the company's stock to fall precipitously. This directly hurts the retirement security of ordinary Americans. In CalPERS case, we're talking about clerks, custodians, school bus drivers, firefighters, and highway repair people, for example.

Since this issue has come to light, an unprecedented number of late filings with the SEC have occurred, which of course, delays disclosure to shareowners.

Secondly, these late filings are often considered to be technical violations of the conditions of borrowing, and that is costing companies too.

Last month, the Wall Street Journal reported that some bondholders are calling in their loans or demanding payment or large fees in exchange for an extension of their default deadlines. As many as two dozen companies were reported to have faced this dilemma over the past 18 months, and some had to pay multi-million dollar fees.

Even more astonishing, as the Wall Street Journal also reported, we are now learning that as stocks sank after the terrorist attacks of September 11, scores of companies rushed to issue options to top tier executives when the stock market had reached its post-attack low on September 21, 2001.

Now comes a cascade of class action and shareowner derivative lawsuits.

Once again, this scandal has brought back a number of fundamental corporate governance questions, such as:

- Are Boards condoning this behavior?
- If not—and the Boards are themselves surprised to learn of questionable backdating—then the question is where was their oversight?
- It raises questions about adequate internal and external auditor controls? Are the auditors being vigorous enough in their examination of a company's option granting practices?

- And finally, investors want to know if illegalities are occurring, will the wrongdoers be swiftly and aggressively prosecuted, and will they be held accountable with civil and criminal penalties where appropriate?

Mr. Chairman, you hit the nail on the head when you said that if the public is to maintain full confidence in our public markets, the appropriate action need to occur.

Over the last two months, we have approached 42 portfolio companies under investigation by the SEC. We have asked that companies perform independent investigations and that they publicly disclose all findings resulting from such investigations, regardless of the outcome.

We have urged company boards of directors to develop policies that disclose how stock option grant dates are established and then publicly disclose those policies in company financial and proxy statements.

We want Company Boards and Compensation Committees to conduct an audit of their executive compensation plan administrator to be sure they are acting in full compliance with their directives.

And we strongly believe something needs to be done to be sure that company resources are *not* used to satisfy the tax and legal liability of executives implicated for this kind of wrongdoing. Such an inappropriate use of corporate assets hurts shareowners twice – once by the fruits of such backdating, and the other when they are allowed to use company assets to defend their actions.

We urge the Committee to call on the SEC to continue to investigate, and to aggressively prosecute wrongdoing.

We believe the SEC has the authority it needs to solve this problem. But we think they need to be more aggressive in enforcing rules for the filing of Forms 3, 4 and 5. SEC rules require company stock sales to be reported on SEC Forms within two days of the date of execution. SEC rules also require two-day reporting of certain transactions between employee benefit plans by officers and directors and that transactions involving stock options such as grants, awards, cancellations and re-pricing be reported in the same time frame.

We welcome the Public Accounting Standards Board's help by providing greater oversight of auditing practices pertaining to option grants. Their July 28th practice alert is very beneficial, and we welcome their continued oversight.

I would like to close by giving our view of the issue of spring loading of options.

We believe the SEC's requirement that an issuer disclose its option grants policy will have a positive effect. It should mitigate the activity of spring loading options in the future. However, should this not prove to be the case, we recommend that the SEC take additional steps to ensure that option grant practices are carried out in a systematic fashion, unaffected by the timing and release of material nonpublic information.

To sum up, we are going to do our part as active shareowners to hold Boards of Directors and Compensation Committees accountable. We will work with the SEC and the PCAOB in whatever way they deem helpful, and of course, we stand ready to assist this Committee by providing additional information. Finally, on behalf of the 1.4 million public servants we represent, I want to thank you once again, Mr. Chairman for all that you and this Committee are doing to restore the public trust in our financial markets.

I would be pleased to answer any questions.

In: Backdating of Stock Options
Editor: Bernard T. Weinstein
ISBN: 978-1-60741-984-6


*Chapter 7*

# STOCK OPTIONS BACKDATING HEARING—SCHACT TESTIMONY

*Kurt N. Schacht*

## INTRODUCTION

I am Kurt Schacht, the Executive Director of the CFA Centre for Financial Market Integrity, the advocacy arm of CFA Institute. I would like to thank Senator Shelby, Senator Sarbanes and other members of this committee for the opportunity to speak to you today on the topic of stock option practices, in particular backdating of option grants. This issue raises important shareholder concerns and we are supportive of your committee taking a closer look, as well as the work of Chairman Cox and the Securities and Exchange Commission (SEC) to investigate alleged abuses.

First, some background about CFA Centre and its parent organization, CFA Institute. CFA Institute is a non-profit professional membership organization with over 84,000 members in 128 countries. Its mission is to lead the investment profession globally by setting the highest standards of ethics, education, and professional excellence. CFA Institute is most widely recognized as the organization that administers the CFA examination and awards the CFA designation, a designation that I share with nearly 68,000 investment professionals worldwide. I direct the advocacy efforts of CFA Institute through the newly created CFA Centre for Financial Market Integrity, which develops research, education projects and promotes ethical standards within the investment industry.

## THE CFA CENTRE PERSPECTIVE: OPTIONS BACKDATING

Our organization approaches this topic primarily as an investor advocate with a focus on protecting shareholder interests and ensuring accurate and transparent financial reporting. We were an early voice for the SEC to amend its newly released executive compensation disclosures to deal with the practice of option backdating and its companion practice of "spring-loading." Both have been prevalent for years and have generally gone unnoticed. In some cases, these practices have been purposefully hidden from shareholder view. The recent focus by various academic studies and the resulting regulatory investigations into the backdating practices have confirmed what is at best, the latest executive compensation controversy and at worst, a growing financial reporting scandal.

Historically, the rationale for granting stock options to executives and other employees was to align their interests with shareowners, and to provide an incentive for them to enhance shareholder value. Several commentators have suggested that even backdated options continue to have such attributes and that the backdating controversy is overblown with politics and rhetoric. They would have us believe it is a "victimless" infraction. In our view, the practices of backdating and spring-loading are unethical manipulations of the option granting process designed to increase employees' compensation to the detriment of shareowners. These practices have been secretive and have placed numerous companies at significant financial and leadership risk. As with most company scandals resulting in significant cost and uncertainty, it is the public shareowners that fall victim.

We remain concerned about the ultimate scope of the backdating problem. Specifically, is this activity limited to the 100-plus firms under formal investigation or does it extend to a much larger group? For a variety of reasons, including the recent public outrage, the requirements of FASB Statement 123R and APB Opinion 25, the Sarbanes Oxley requirement to file accelerated Form 4's and the new SEC compensation disclosure rules, backdating itself may be yesterday's problem. However, the degree of necessary "clean-up" due to the vast number of companies and the size of stock options incentives in 1990-2002, seems to be unknown. It represents an overhang for individual companies for sure, but more problematic, it must not become a sequel to the lost confidence in financial reporting experienced earlier in this decade.

One mitigating factor may be that in recent months, the use of stock options has fallen out of favor due partly to the new option expensing rules. Whether we consider long term effects or short term effects of backdating and spring-loading, options use has become more rationalized. What this may signal however, is a need for further examination of the "replacement" for options, the practice of granting restricted stock. We should be certain that the gaming of grant dates or material information has not become part of the calculus for this now more favored type of stock incentive.

One final point of perspective relates to the ethical implications of backdating. This controversy comes at a time when executive compensation practices in general, are under intense scrutiny. These latest revelations concerning backdating and spring-loading certainly appear to be yet more practices intentionally conducted under the radar, for obvious reasons. It leaves many wondering about the respective standards and duties of officers and directors who approved of and even participated in some of these option granting irregularities. This is all the more troubling given that the practice appears to have continued after Sarbanes Oxley was passed in 2002 and suggests that at least some compensation and audit committee members may have been less than diligent in their duties.

## ACCOUNTING AND AUDITING PRACTICE - WHAT HAPPENED?

The accounting standard relating to stock option expenses that existed for many years before FASB Statement 123R was clear. APB Opinion 25 allowed companies to avoid a compensation expense only if certain criteria were met. Such criteria clearly included a requirement that the underlying stock price on the date of the grant must be equal to the exercise price of the options. Stated differently, the grant date price and the exercise price must match, in order to avoid the attendant compensation expense.

It is difficult to fashion an argument as to how this might ever happen in the context of backdating an option grant. Therefore, in nearly every case where an option grant date was backdated, a compensation expense was required to be recognized and reported in the company's income statement, unless it was deemed immaterial. As a result, nearly every company identified in the press as having backdating problems failed to properly record compensation expense for options and thereby filed financial statements that did not comply with the U.S. Generally Accepted Accounting Principles (GAAP) (again, unless the amount of expense was "immaterial").

Viewing this in the context of external auditor responsibilities, it remains unclear how this practice was repeatedly missed or worse, sanctioned. In some cases it may have been sloppiness, incompetence or both. In other cases it may have been an intentional act of concealment by the responsible managers. A number of the accounting firms have suggested that the client company's option documentation was typically taken at face value. Such documentation would generally indicate that the company had granted at-the-money, fixed-plan, employee options, when in fact they had not. This "papering" of the option transactions therefore appeared as though no compensation cost needed to be reported.

Generally, auditors thought that option practice was a low-risk (non cash) area and relied on the client company's records without attempting to verify if such records reflected what actually occurred. We think a clear lesson has now been established. However, we remain concerned whether auditors were actually complicit, turning a blind eye because of client pressures or because it seemed like "every one was doing it" (backdating). We have little doubt that auditors today will acknowledge that backdating typically failed to meet the criteria of APB Opinion 25, that is, recognition of zero expense only for at-the-money options.

It is now the case in over 100 countries around the world that follow either U.S. GAAP or International Accounting Standards rules, that backdating, without *expensing of the full fair value of the options*, would constitute a violation of accounting standards. Whether because of these new option expensing rules, Sarbanes Oxley, the public furor over backdating or some combination thereof, we must now expect that proper audit procedures would demand a closer look and verification of these options and restricted stock practices. We expect this will be facilitated by the SEC's new executive compensation disclosure requirements.

## LINGERING CONCERNS

As we noted above, the companion practice of spring-loading options grants should be further scrutinized. This involves the gaming of grants around the release of material non-public information. Studies suggest this has been rampant for many years and it happens regardless of whether grant dates are fixed annually or at the discretion of management or directors. The protections offered by the Sarbanes Oxley accelerated Form 4 filing, does not address this. While the latest executive compensation disclosure requirements of the SEC do require a full review and report by the compensation committee on any spring-loading activities, it does not prohibit them. We would encourage a closer look at whether officers and directors in control of the option granting process should be barred from participating in any spring-loaded grants, just as they would be prohibited from trading in any other company securities while in the possession of inside information.

We have one additional concern. We believe that one facilitator of backdating was accounting rules that failed to result in fair value expensing of the cost of the options. As we have said, auditors apparently failed to consider such off-balance-sheet (OBS) items of sufficiently high risk to warrant full scrutiny and thorough audits of the option grants. Many more items, several of considerable size relative to most companies' balance sheets, remain off-balance-sheet and unexpensed, and reported if at all, in the notes. We would hope that auditors would learn from the lessons of the 2001-2002 corporate collapses involving large OBS transactions and the backdating/spring-loading problems currently receiving scrutiny and tighten their procedures to make certain that these receive the same attention as items required to be expensed.

## CONCLUSION

We commend the members of the Committee for your continued attention and leadership on this unethical industry practice. In summary, we encourage three further steps.

- Consideration of a possible ban on spring loading for named executives and directors.
- A closer look by auditors and regulators for any irregularities in the granting process used for restricted stock.

- A bolstering of audit procedures to include a closer review of any other off balance sheet items posing similar risks of being misreported.

Our markets can ill afford further lapses in the ethics relating to executive compensation or the integrity of financial reporting. We have been down that market–paralyzing road before.

# INDEX

## A



## B



## C

## J



## L



## M



## N



## O



## P

## R



## S

## T



## U



## V